MW00800648

## PRAISE FOR THE PBIS CHAMPION MODEL

"The Champion Model System has brought profound changes to the way we think about student behavior management in Central Unified. Data is utilized within a problem-solving framework in order to improve the outcomes of students. Through the Champion Model System, schools have developed innovative, creative, and functional ways of implementing PBIS behavioral supports. It has brought greater visibility and awareness of the need to develop political support, parent involvement, and funding strategies to support PBIS. Small group interventions have been put in place to monitor and support students with particular behavioral needs. The Champion Model System has helped create a culture of academic and behavior success for all students."

Kevin Wagner
*Interim Assistant Superintendent, Human Resources*
*Central Unified School District*

"The PBIS Champion Model has made such an incredible difference in the lives of the most needy students. Students who normally would be at home are now in the classroom where they belong. This model allows students to understand what they did wrong and what they will do so the behavior is never repeated."

Dr. Wesley Sever
*Superintendent*
*Kingsburg Elementary Charter School District*

"It has been great for our schools and district to be motivated and recognized for their hard work in providing innovative and creative ways to support all students."

Matthew Navo
*Superintendent*
*Sanger Unified School District*

"The PBIS Champion Model has been instrumental in creating a tangible and positive climate and culture shift in our schools. Not only can you see it in action, you can feel it when you step on a campus. When suspensions and expulsions drop to zero at some school sites you know PBIS has undeniably changed the way we define and respond to behavior. Students are better for it, staff loves it, and our parents ask about how to replicate at home. You can't ask for anything better than that."

Kimberly Salomonson
*Director of Pupil Services*
*Sanger Unified School District*

"The PBIS Champion Model provided a framework for Central Unified School District that improved our support systems and procedures and provided clear behavior expectations for all students and staff. It continues to have a major impact on the culture of our schools and community. The results were so significant we will be implementing PBIS district-wide in Paso Robles."

Chris Williams
*Superintendent*
*Paso Robles Unified School District*

"The staff development we have received through the Champion Model has been exemplary. It has provided the support and training our sites need in order to fully realize a highly engaging school climate for our students. The support tools provide a valued resource for our site leadership, and when combined with the training information, provide a comprehensive support system for our district to maximize our efforts in promoting a positive school climate."

Mimi Bonds
*Director, Student Services*
*Visalia Unified School District*

"The PBIS Champion Model System has provided schools an effective way to collect data on behavior while simultaneously making a positive impact on the culture of a school. It has transformed schools and inspired educators to have a positive approach to behavior on their campuses."

Erik Nyberg
*Program Manager*
*Fresno County Office of Education*

"The PBIS Champion Model System has had a far reaching effect on the schools, students, and families served by Fresno County Office of Education. This system has given our schools a new way to look at positive discipline and its impact on academic success."

Trina Frazier
*Administrator, SELPA/Special Education*
*Fresno County Office of Education*

# The PBIS Tier One Handbook

## A Practical Approach to Implementing the Champion Model

Jessica Djabrayan Hannigan
Linda Hauser

CORWIN
A SAGE Company

FOR INFORMATION:

Corwin

A SAGE Company

2455 Teller Road

Thousand Oaks, California 91320

(800) 233-9936

www.corwin.com

SAGE Publications Ltd.

1 Oliver's Yard

55 City Road

London EC1Y 1SP

United Kingdom

SAGE Publications India Pvt. Ltd.

B 1/I 1 Mohan Cooperative Industrial Area

Mathura Road, New Delhi 110 044

India

SAGE Publications Asia-Pacific Pte. Ltd.

3 Church Street

#10-04 Samsung Hub

Singapore 049483

Acquisitions Editor:  Jessica Allan

Associate Editor:  Kimberly Greenberg

Editorial Assistant:  Cesar Reyes

Production Editor:  Veronica Stapleton
Hooper

Copy Editor:  Megan Markanich

Typesetter:  C&M Digitals (P) Ltd.

Proofreader:  Ellen Howard

Indexer:  Sheila Bodell

Cover Designer:  Michael Dubowe

Marketing Manager:  Amanda Boudria

Copyright © 2015 by Corwin

All rights reserved. When forms and sample documents are included, their use is authorized only by educators, local school sites, and/or noncommercial or nonprofit entities that have purchased the book. Except for that usage, no part of this book may be reproduced or utilized in any form or by any means, electronic or mechanical, including photocopying, recording, or by any information storage and retrieval system, without permission in writing from the publisher.

All trademarks depicted within this book, including trademarks appearing as part of a screenshot, figure, or other image, are included solely for the purpose of illustration and are the property of their respective holders. The use of the trademarks in no way indicates any relationship with, or endorsement by, the holders of said trademarks.

Printed in the United States of America

*Library of Congress Cataloging-in-Publication Data*

Djabrayan Hannigan, Jessica.

The PBIS tier one handbook : a practical approach to implementing the champion model / Jessica Djabrayan Hannigan, Linda Hauser.

pages cm
Includes bibliographical references and index.

ISBN 978-1-4833-7557-1 (pbk. : alk. paper)

1. School psychology—United States. 2. Behavior modification—United States. 3. School children—United States—Discipline. 4. Students—United States—Psychology. 5. School management and organization—United States. I. Hauser, Linda. II. Title.

LB1060.2.D53 2015
370.15'28—dc          232015011252

This book is printed on acid-free paper.

19 20 21 22 12 11 10 9

# Contents

# Preface

We wrote this book because we believe in the 85/15 rule associated with school improvement, which states that 85 percent of the problems in a system are due to inherent problems with the system. Schools can change these problems only through the actions of the people who shape the system—our educational leaders such as policy makers, superintendents, principals, and teachers. In other words, blame the system, not the kids.

We believe in the fundamental goodness of our children. We contend that each student upon entering the educational system desires and intends to be successful academically, socially, and emotionally. The long-standing deficit thinking, "wait-to-fail" educational model has actually contributed to and in many instances caused dysfunction and poor performance in our schools. We deeply believe that every child can be successful if provided the right conditions—a proactive model designed to create a system for great first teaching, high levels of learning, and an environment where students and adults thrive.

We understand the challenges in creating such systems. Prior to implementing our proactive model, we heard many educator voices across the nation communicate concern about the current ability of school systems to create environments where every child learns and conditions that bring out each student's best. Do any of these messages resonate with you?

> *"The administrators don't do anything about discipline at our school."*

> *"I do not know how to handle this student or class."*

> *"We do not have the time, resources, or personnel to do alternative discipline at our school."*

> *"Some students are just bad."*

> *"I do not have time to fill out all these forms."*

*"Nothing will work for these students. It is not worth it."*

*"Their parents should be teaching them how to behave, not us."*

*"We are a zero tolerance school."*

*"That kid is going to end up in jail anyway."*

*"We have the highest number of suspensions in our district because we do not tolerate bad behavior."*

*"These interventions won't work for the students in our school."*

*"This class is out of control."*

*"I don't want this kid back in my class, and I have a right to suspend him."*

These statements are indicators first of a system issue, not a kid problem. As Edward Demings once stated, *every system is perfectly designed to get the results it is getting.* In order to change outcomes, you have to change the system that is producing these undesirable results.

We are in an unprecedented time in educational history—one of challenge, great opportunity, and enormous possibility for a profound and positive future. We must work smarter, and this smart work begins with looking at our system. Our students deserve nothing less than a high-quality system—a system that brings out their very best academically, socially, and emotionally. That is why we developed the framework for a Positive Behavior Interventions and Supports (PBIS) Champion Model System.

We believe it is our responsibility as educators to design a system that will bring out each student's best, and we encourage all educators to start with a look at your system. This practical resource will guide you in your efforts to create quality environments in schools and districts that optimize learning and build a solid Tier 1 PBIS system. On behalf of the millions of students across the nation, and especially for the students you are entrusted to teach and lead every day, we need your help to change the traditional mind-set and develop a proactive approach for the future. If you accept this challenge and incredible opportunity to make a systemic and systematic change in your school and district, read on!

# Acknowledgments

## JESSICA'S ACKNOWLEDGMENTS

I wish to personally thank the following people and organizations for their contributions to my inspiration and knowledge and for other help in creating this book: Fresno County Office of Education PBIS training team and administration; Central Unified School District family; all Fresno County and non–Fresno County School Districts I have trained and am currently training; my Polk Elementary School family; and all my direct supervisors, mentors, professors, students, friends, and family members who allowed me to innovate and be passionate about what I believed in. This would have not been possible without all of you.

To my immediate family—Mom, Dad, Johnny, Joey, Vero, Liam, Nene, and Pera—I could have not completed this book without your endless love and support. Furthermore, a special thank-you goes to my father, Bedros, and mother, Dzovinar, who left everything they had in their home country of Lebanon to give me and my brothers, Johnny and Joey, the safety, security, and opportunity to receive the education we needed to succeed in life. Without the relentless support of my parents, I would not be able to have the courage, strength, confidence, and tenacity to pursue my goals and dreams.

Thank you to my smart, thoughtful, and loving stepdaughters, Rowan and Riley, for always encouraging and supporting me throughout this process. I hope to model for you what it means to never give up, have high expectations for yourselves and others, and make your dreams come true.

To my husband, John, you inspire me every day as a husband, father, best friend, and colleague. You are the epitome of an administrator of a Gold PBIS Champion Model School. The impact you have on everyone who sets foot on your school campus and your continued contributions to the field of education motivate me to never stop advocating and helping all students. My dream is for all administrators to have the passion, dedication, and drive to innovate and provide the best for all students, staff, and families as you do.

My appreciation goes to the team at Corwin Press for recognizing that this is a comprehensive system for behavior and is a need for schools throughout the nation. Thank you for giving me the platform to share my voice and help students.

A special thank you goes to my coauthor, colleague, and friend Linda Hauser for believing in my vision and helping me create a system that can have a timeless impact on students and schools. Thank you for being on this journey with me.

To all who decide to read this book, I thank you for joining our PBIS Champion Model System family and doing what is best for students.

## LINDA'S ACKNOWLEDGMENTS

I would like to thank two very important families—my personal family and professional family—who have greatly influenced my life. First, I would like to acknowledge and thank my personal family beginning with the love of my life, Rob, my husband of 35 years, who has always put our children and me first. Thank you for always being there and making it possible for me to pursue each and every dream (mother of two children while serving as a principal, earning numerous credentials as well as master's and doctoral degrees, serving in many district leadership roles, and now a university professor). Thank you, Kelly and Jeffrey, my two grown children, who have taught me so much about life and love since the day you were born. You have brought such joy to my life. To my mother, Charlotte, three sisters and brother (Carla, Sandy, Gail, and Steve), sister-in-law and brothers-in-law (Karen, Richard, and Paul), son-in-law (Shawn), nieces and nephews (Jeanette, Deanna, Lindsey, Eric, David, Michael, Mathew, Lauren, Robbie, and Sam), great nieces and nephews (Joseph, Jeremy, Taylor, Paige, and Gavin), thank you for your continual support, encouragement, and unconditional love. Thank you to my father, Carl, who went to be with the Lord twenty years ago, and who always believed I could do anything and everything. He would be looking down on us now saying, "That's my girl." To the little men in my life, and two very precious gifts from God, my grandsons, James (3 years) and Zachary (1 year), you are a daily reminder of why I do what I do. If any of you want to know the true meaning of family, then you need to meet mine.

I would also like to acknowledge my professional family, the Clovis Unified School District (25 years), the Fresno Unified School District (3 years), and my current education family at Fresno State, especially my colleagues in the Department of Educational Leadership, and the schools of the Central Valley, where I have learned and continue to learn so much about teaching, learning, and leadership.

Last, but certainly not least, I would like to acknowledge my former student and now colleague, thinking partner, and coauthor of this book, Jessica. Thank you for inviting me on this journey with you. It has been exciting, rewarding, and quite a learning experience.

## PUBLISHER'S ACKNOWLEDGMENTS

Corwin gratefully acknowledges the contributions of the following reviewers:

Jennifer Betters-Bubon

Assistant Professor

University of Wisconsin–Whitewater

Whitewater, WI

Katy Olweiler

Counselor

Lakeside School

Seattle, WA

Roberto Pamas

Principal

Oliver Wendell Holmes Middle School

Alexandria, VA

Franciene Sabens, M.S. Ed., LPC, NCC

Professional School Counselor

Chester High School

Chester, IL

This book is dedicated with love and affection
to the students of today and tomorrow,
who deserve a quality environment for
unlimited learning and a future of endless possibilities.

*And also to Liam, Rowan, Riley, James, & Zachary*

# About the Authors

**Dr. Jessica Djabrayan Hannigan** is the Supervisor of Student Support Services in Central Unified School District, Fresno, California. She is a graduate of the University of California, Los Angeles (UCLA). She holds a master's in school psychology and a doctorate in educational leadership. She is an adjunct professor in the Educational Leadership Department at California State University, Fresno. She is also an educational consultant working with several school districts and county offices in California on designing and implementing effective behavior systems in schools and districts that work. Dr. Hannigan currently trains approximately 300 schools on the Positive Behavior Interventions and Supports (PBIS) Champion Model System, which is the model system she designed based on her doctoral research and experiences in working with a variety of schools and districts. Her focus is on teaching teachers, administrators, and support staff how to create behavior systems in schools similar to academic systems. Dr. Hannigan resides in Fresno, California, with her husband, John, and her two stepdaughters, Rowan and Riley.

**Dr. Linda Hauser** has been deeply involved in education for over thirty-five years. She is a professor at California State University, Fresno, where she teaches in both the Educational Leadership and Administration (principal preparation) program and the Doctoral Program in Educational Leadership, as well as serves as department chair, program coordinator, and dissertation adviser. Prior to her tenure as a university professor, Dr. Hauser served over twenty-eight years in California public education as the chief academic officer for the Fresno Unified School District and as an area superintendent, administrator for professional development, elementary school principal, secondary learning director, resource teacher, and teacher in the Clovis Unified School District. She has taught numerous grade ranges from primary grade students to the graduate level. Dr. Hauser received her bachelor's degree in communicative disorders (deaf education emphasis) and teaching credential from California State University, Fresno; her master's in administration and reading specialist credential from Fresno Pacific University; and completed a doctorate in educational leadership from the University of La Verne. Under Dr. Hauser's leadership as elementary principal, her school was recognized as a National Blue Ribbon School. She has done and continues to do extensive work in schools and districts in organizational development and facilitation as a new leadership competency; system's alignment; teaching, learning, and instructional leadership for high performance; and developing and implementing tiered systems of interventions and support. Dr. Hauser delivers numerous presentations at national and state conferences, is an author of peer-reviewed articles, and was an award recipient from the National Staff Development Council (NSDC) for a model professional development program: Project BEST (Beginning Educator's Support in Teaching). Linda lives in Fresno, California, with her husband, Rob, of thirty-five years. They are proud parents and grandparents. Their grown daughter, Kelly, and her husband, Shawn, reside in Carlsbad, California, with their two precious grandsons, James and Zachary. Grown son Jeffrey resides in Newport Beach, California.

# The What and Why of PBIS

**O**ver decades of educating our youth, we have all heard it stated in one way or another that *in order for students to learn, they need an environment that is conducive to learning.* Research has shown that schools can make a significant positive impact on their students regardless of their circumstance. At the heart of Lezotte's (2010) effective schools research, seven factors were identified as characteristics of effective schools across the racial and socioeconomic spectrum. The first factor had to do with creating a school environment where students feel safe emotionally and physically—a climate free of behaviors such as bullying, fighting, harassing—in an environment not created merely through punishment. Michael Thompson (Fabelo et al., 2011), researcher and director of the Justice Center at the Council of State Governments, conducted a study indicating that the discipline of suspension and expulsion for "discretionary violations" actually does more harm than good for the individual student. This type of discipline damages the sense of community within the school, and students are three times more likely to end up in a juvenile detention center the following year if they receive suspensions and expulsions for discretionary violations. Thompson advocates for school-wide implementation of "positive behavior interventions and supports" to prevent misbehavior.

Through our work in hundreds of schools, we have encountered and experienced school environments or aspects of the school environment described in School Environment A and School Environment B. Which of

| School Environment A | School Environment B |
|---|---|
| ✓ As students arrive to campus, there is no evidence of adults welcoming and greeting students. | ✓ With your first step on the campus, you feel so welcomed that you feel like you belong; the positive culture is contagious. |
| ✓ Walls are bare with just a few signs indicating where the office and bathrooms are located. | ✓ Positively stated messages are posted in every setting throughout the school. |
| ✓ Upon entering the school office, no one acknowledges you for several minutes, and when spoken to, it is with a negative or irritated tone. | ✓ Upon entering the school office, school personnel greet you, and you feel like you are their priority. |
| ✓ Staff and students are unclear about behavior expectations. The main message communicated to students is *what not to do*. | ✓ Clear behavior expectations and rules are evident and understood by all students and staff. The main message communicated to students is *what to do*. |
| ✓ The office is filled with students lined up to see an administrator for misconduct. However, staff members complain that nothing ever happens to students sent to the office for misconduct. | ✓ Office referrals are minimal. More students are lined up in the office being acknowledged for appropriate expected behavior. |
| ✓ Negative talk about students, administration, and/or other colleagues permeates the staff lounge. | ✓ Productive talk permeates the staff lounge. It is a family atmosphere of caring and sharing. |
| ✓ Students take their time getting to class after the bell rings, unconcerned about being tardy or missing instruction. | ✓ Students understand the value of being to class on time and don't want to miss a minute of instruction. |
| ✓ Administrators are consumed with discipline issues all day long; therefore, it is difficult for them to get out of their offices. | ✓ Teachers greet students daily as they walk into the classroom with a handshake, high five, fist pump, or positive verbal acknowledgment. Active supervision of students occurs in designated locations throughout the schools. |

the two school environments or parts of the environment most resonate with you? Which environment would you like to experience every day?

Abundant research supports what we all now know: As educators, we must create a school environment that results in a positive impact on the emotional, social, and physical well-being of every child and accelerates learning. So now what? How do we take this knowledge and translate it into action? How many of us at either a district or school level have been or are expected to design and sustain a tiered system for support for the other side of the triangle—the social, emotional, and behavioral support side—but are a little unclear about what that might look and sound like? Where is the comprehensive book that supports educators in bridging this knowledge-implementation gap, and guides us in how to create a system that every one of our students deserves—a Positive Behavior Interventions and Supports (PBIS) Champion Model System? Until this book, one did not exist.

The foundation for this book was built on the original dissertation research work of Dr. Jessica Djabrayan Hannigan in partnership with Dr. Linda Hauser and on years of putting this research into everyday practice where it matters most—in schools and districts positively changing the lives of kids. For schools that have implemented our PBIS Champion Model System, academic and behavioral results have not only been positive but profound and compelling. Schools have seen a 50 percent or more decrease in discipline incidents during their first year of implementation, which have resulted in more students staying in school, less student and adult time and energy spent on behavior issues with more time and energy spent on learning, and more resources allocated toward the mental health of students requiring Tier 2 and Tier 3 supports (preventive model).

The two authors of this book have a combined fifty plus years of experience learning from and leading students, community members, teachers, principals, university partners, and district office staff. Dr. Jessica Djabrayan Hannigan has recently trained over 300 schools in California on the PBIS Champion Model System. The primary purpose of this book is to share from our research, study, experience, and practice what we have learned about designing, implementing, and sustaining highly effective PBIS systems that produce positive academic and behavioral outcomes in schools. Our ultimate goal is to support teachers, schools, and districts in creating positive learning environments where students and adults thrive and experience academic and social success. This book is intended to be an interactive guide—a how-to for practitioners—in creating quality environments in schools and districts that optimize learning and build a solid Tier 1 PBIS system.

## WHAT IS PBIS?

PBIS is a systems approach to establish the social culture and the behavioral supports needed for all children in a school to achieve both social and academic success (Sugai & Horner, 2002). PBIS is not a new intervention package or a theory of behavior. It is the application of a behaviorally based systems approach to enhance the capacity of schools, families, and communities to design and facilitate effective environments where teaching and learning can occur. Designed to develop a culture of positive behavior support in schools, the implementation of a PBIS system is intended to create an environment for great first teaching, high levels of learning, and improved behavior within general and special education classroom settings.

We design systems to teach students to read and do math as well as teach children and young adults how to tie their shoes, ride a bike, and drive a car; however, we sometimes fail to explicitly teach students how to behave or the actions needed to create an environment that fosters their success. Why is this? Do we believe we do not have enough time during the school day or that focusing our energy and time in this area will take away critical instructional time for academics? Do we believe this is the parent's responsibility? Do we assume that students should and do know the expected behaviors in all educational settings? Research shows that schools using traditional types of discipline continue to experience significant increases in violence and destructive behavior as well as increases in the number of students excluded from instruction due to suspension or expulsion. Furthermore, the use of suspension and expulsion in schools is negatively related to academic achievement independent of socioeconomic influences; and exclusionary discipline such as office referrals, suspensions, and expulsions does not contribute to better learning outcomes (Skiba & Rausch, 2005). As Einstein stated, the definition of insanity is "doing the same thing over and over again and expecting different results." We must be focused on results, not just emotions. The old way of doing business to address student behavior is not working. We can no longer accept or afford the wait-to-fail or wait-to-misbehave model of behavior; we must be proactive.

A more proactive approach to implementing efficacious behavior supports includes such actions as consistently using and reviewing discipline policies within the classroom and school (Fenning & Bohanon, 2006), developing a discipline team (Noonan, Tunney, Fogal, & Sarich, 1999), and using data to evaluate discipline codes (Sugai & Horner, 2002). Therefore, many states, school districts, and schools have shifted from a wait-to-misbehave approach that is followed by an attempt to change student behavior through punishment or through a high negative impact consequence model to implementation of school-wide prevention and proactive approaches such as PBIS.

## HOW IS PBIS CONNECTED TO RESPONSE TO INTERVENTION?

Similar to Response to Intervention (RTI), the PBIS framework follows a three-tiered system of intervention delivery, providing different levels of behavior support based on student need and response to the intervention. If the student is not responsive to the intervention in the primary tier (Tier 1), more intensive behavioral intervention is provided in the secondary tier (Tier 2), or a highly individualized plan is developed for the student who needs more intensive tertiary tier (Tier 3) support. Experience has taught us that the RTI framework is most helpful in understanding and organizing data and student information. Based on how students respond, each intervention tier includes specific implementation elements.

## PBIS PRIMARY TIER (TIER 1)

- Behavioral expectations defined
- Behavioral expectations taught
- Reward system for appropriate behavior
- Continuum of consequences for problem behavior
- Continuous data collection and use for decision making (Horner, Sugai, & Anderson, 2010)

## PBIS SECONDARY TIER (TIER 2)

- Universal screening
- Progress monitoring for at-risk students
- System for increasing structure and predictability
- System for increasing contingent adult feedback
- System for linking academic and behavioral performance
- System for increasing home/school communication
- Data collection and use for decision making (Horner et al., 2010)

## PBIS TERTIARY TIER (TIER 3)

- Functional behavioral assessment
- Team-based comprehensive assessment
- Linking of academic and behavioral supports
- Individualized intervention based on assessment information and focused on: (a) prevention of problem contexts, (b) instruction on functional equivalent skills and desired performance skills, (c) strategies for extinction of problem behavior, (d) strategies for enhancing contingent reward of desired behavior, and (e) use of negative or safety consequences if needed
- Data collection and use for decision making (Horner et al., 2010)

PBIS is implemented in many schools and districts throughout the United States—specifically, in states that have transformed their academic and behavioral practices to improve student achievement. We have found through our years of research, experience, and practice that the schools and districts most effective at PBIS implementation and progress monitoring are implementers who follow quality criteria. As a result of our study and work, we have developed both a framework for creating a comprehensive PBIS model system and accompanying tools, strategies, and action steps to help move classroom, school, and district systems one step closer to designing and implementing a proactive behavior model that produces great results and outcomes for all students. Examples and case studies from several schools implementing PBIS at a Champion Model level are highlighted in this book.

# The PBIS Champion Model System and What Led to Its Development

**W**e were interested in learning practical ways to implement Positive Behavior Interventions and Supports (PBIS) in all types of schools (elementary, secondary, and alternative education settings) and, most importantly, how to develop, support, and sustain a quality PBIS system—a system producing exemplary results. Therefore, our journey began not only with a review of what the literature had to say but with an investigation of PBIS systems throughout the nation to identify and deeply understand the characteristics of an effective system and processes that supported development and sustainability of these systems. This research and extensive study provided the foundation for the development of our framework, the PBIS Champion Model System. Site visits were conducted in schools throughout the country, observing for quality characteristics and examining the positive academic and behavioral outcomes perceived to be to a large extent the result of PBIS implementation.

Recognizing the value in the organization and structure of Florida's Positive Behavior Support (FLPBS) Project (n.d.), we adapted and expanded this work to develop the PBIS Champion Model System, an action-oriented framework designed to guide the development of a PBIS system to Bronze,

Silver, and Gold levels (George, 2008). The focus of this book is on Tier 1—Bronze PBIS Champion Model System implementation. An effective Tier 1 PBIS system meets the behavior needs of at least 80 percent of the student population and lays the foundation for the development and operation of successful Tier 2 and Tier 3 systems—systems designed for students not responding as intended to Tier 1. We believe that if more than 20 percent of the student population has behavior intervention needs beyond Tier 1, the system has a core problem not a behavior intervention problem. Since we also believe that it is critical to understand the *big picture*, all levels of the system, and the importance Tier 1 plays in the larger systems picture, we have included an overview of each Tier of the PBIS Champion Model System framework.

The PBIS Champion Model System (see Figure 2.1) is a framework for creating a comprehensive systems approach for the design and delivery of PBIS at a school. This action-oriented framework provides *quality criteria* and *how-to steps* for developing, implementing, monitoring, and sustaining each level of the system: Bronze (Tier 1), Silver (Tier 2), and Gold (Tier 3). Each tier in the system consists of three categories: Category A–Markers, Category B–Characteristics, and Category C–Academic and

**Figure 2.1**   PBIS Champion Model System

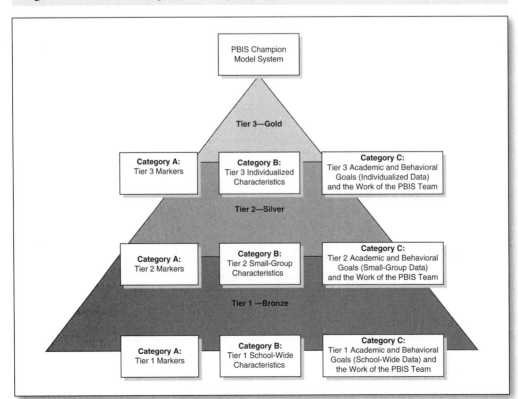

Behavioral Goals and the Work of the PBIS Team. Each category is composed of quality criteria and a set of defined actions. A brief overview of the quality criteria for each tier is provided with a quick glimpse of what a Champion Model school would look like at each level (Bronze, Silver, and Gold).

> *Implementing the PBIS Champion Model System has changed the entire culture of my school.*
>
> —Dr. Lisa Houston, principal

## TIER 1
## Bronze PBIS Champion Model System
## (80 percent of students should respond to this level of support)

- Establish and operate an effective PBIS team.
- Establish and maintain faculty/staff commitment.
- Establish and deploy effective procedures for dealing with discipline.
- Establish a data entry procedure and design an analysis plan.
- Establish a set of school-wide behavior expectations and rules.
- Establish a behavior reward/recognition program.
- Develop and deliver lesson plans for teaching school-wide behavioral expectations and rules.
- Develop and deploy a school-wide PBIS implementation plan.
- Establish classroom systems—routines/procedures.
- Establish and execute an evaluation plan.
- Achieve a score of 80 percent or higher on Benchmarks of Quality (BoQ).
- Achieve an *On Target* score (30–37 points) on the On-Site PBIS Tier 1 Walkthrough Form.
- Demonstrate improvement in school-wide academic and behavioral student outcomes.

### So What Would You See if You Walked into a Bronze PBIS Champion Model School?

If you walked into a school operating at a Bronze level, you would see school-wide behavior expectations posted in all settings; rules articulated by location in every setting; expectations and rules taught and modeled to students in all settings; evidence that students and staff (both classified and certificated) know the school-wide expectations and the school's behavior and reward/recognition systems; a PBIS team, made up of diverse individuals who meet monthly for at least an hour, using a structured agenda, norms, and a follow-up mechanism; an information or data management system for gathering and analyzing behavior data; and then system actions taken based on data.

*I haven't had a suspension at my school since the 2010–2011 school year, and that is a credit to the PBIS Champion Model System. It has completely changed the way our school responds to discipline.*

—Dr. John Hannigan, principal

---

**TIER 2**
**Silver PBIS Champion Model System**
**(Additional support for 10 to 15 percent of students beyond Tier 1 supports)**

---

- Execute all actions and meet all criteria in Tier 1.
- Structure and provide additional small-group teaching opportunities for students not responding to Tier 1 support.
- Establish a Tier 2 PBIS team subgroup, selected from the PBIS team, that meets twice a month to discuss students needing additional support (usually comprised of school psychologist or like position and administration).
- Develop criteria for students needing additional supports (number of office discipline referrals, suspensions, teacher input and observation, etc.).
- Design structured day and recess plans for students in need of more structured time, and actively supervise to ensure safety of Tier 2 students and others.
- Identify check-in/check-out person(s) who connect with Tier 2 intervention student(s) needing additional support at the beginning and end of each day.
- Establish counseling groups aligned with identified student behavior needs. Use counseling groups to teach targeted behaviors (oftentimes conducted by the school psychologist, school counselor, or similar position).
- Closely monitor behavioral and academic data of students receiving Tier 2 interventions.
- Achieve a score of 80 percent or higher on Benchmarks of Quality (BoQ).
- Achieve an *On Target* score (30–37 points) on the On-Site PBIS Tier 1 Walkthrough Form.
- Achieve a score of 80 percent or higher on Benchmarks for Advanced Tiers (BAT) or Monitoring Advanced Tiers Tool (MATT)—Tier 2.
- Demonstrate improvement in small-group academic and behavioral student outcomes.

---

**So What Would You See if You Walked into a Silver PBIS Champion Model School?**

If you walked into a school operating at a Silver level, you would see everything mentioned in the Bronze level school, but now the PBIS team and staff are digging deeper into the behavior data and have established entry and exit criteria for their Tier 2 behavior intervention programs such as Check-In Check-Out (CICO). A school at this level has a staff that is able to articulate the Tier 2 behavior intervention programs available at the school to help students not responding to the Tier 1 system. In addition, a Tier 2 data collection and progress monitoring system such as School-Wide Information System (SWIS) with access to the CICO component is effectively operating, and the staff uses information from this system to identify and provide appropriate Tier 2 interventions as well as monitors for students that are both responding and not responding to the interventions.

*The PBIS Champion Model System has allowed us to create a system for effective discipline that changes behaviors.*

—Jack Kelejian, principal

## TIER 3
## Gold PBIS Champion Model System
## (Additional support for 3 to 5 percent of students beyond Tier 1 and Tier 2 supports)

- Execute all actions and meet all criteria in Tier 1 and Tier 2.
- Establish a Tier 3 PBIS team subgroup—selected from the PBIS team—that meets twice a month to discuss students needing additional support (Tier 2 team subgroup usually serves in this capacity as well).
- School psychologist or a similar position provides individualized counseling supports based on specific behavior needs of the student.
- School psychologist or a similar position designs practical and effective formal and informal behavior support plans with input from all stakeholders and helps monitor progress of behavior support plan implementation.
- School psychologist or a similar position and school administration support families in making sure that medical behavior needs are met, if applicable.
- Consider, if appropriate, special education testing by the special education team.
- Provide wraparound services support at home and school (school psychologist or a similar position and administration research county, university, and other available community programs that can provide additional support in partnership with the school and parents).
- Monitor the progress of Tier 3 intervention students, daily or weekly, with ongoing communication between parents, teachers, and administration.
- Refer students for an alternative setting, if appropriate, and based on the severity of behavioral needs.
- Achieve a score of 80 percent or higher on Benchmarks of Quality (BoQ).

*(Continued)*

(Continued)

- Achieve an *On Target* score (30–37 points) on the On-Site PBIS Tier 1 Walkthrough Form.
- Achieve a score of 80 percent or higher on Benchmarks for Advanced Tiers (BAT) or Monitoring Advanced Tiers Tool (MATT)—Tier 3.
- Demonstrate improvement in individualized academic and behavioral student outcomes.

> **So What Would You See if You Walked into a Gold PBIS Champion Model School?**
>
> If you walked into a school operating at a Gold level, you would see everything mentioned in schools operating at the Silver level, but now the PBIS team and staff have established criteria for identifying and supporting students not responding to Tier 1 or Tier 2 interventions. In a Gold school, all staff members clearly articulate the importance of understanding factors that may trigger problem student behavior and are equipped with the skills and resources to support students needing more intensive support academically and behaviorally. A Tier 3 PBIS team has been established and works on analyzing and adjusting behavior interventions for an individualized system. The information or data management system has the capability to design individualized data-monitoring charts along with specific indicators. In addition, teachers and administrators use alternative discipline approaches that focus on changing behaviors.

The remainder of this book focuses on how to design, implement, and operate a Bronze PBIS Champion Model System, which establishes a solid Tier 1 PBIS foundation for system success at all levels. We contend that PBIS is not operating at your school if, at minimum, the Tier 1 Bronze Champion Model System categories are not in place. The Bronze PBIS Champion Model System is designed to help you build a strong Tier 1 PBIS foundation, focused on meeting the needs of at least 80 percent of your student population. In order to operate at this level, you will learn the ABCs to success, which are illustrated in Figure 2.2:

Category A: Tier 1—Ten PBIS Markers

Category B: Tier 1—Four School-Wide Characteristics

Category C: Tier 1—School-Wide Academic and Behavioral Goals and the Work of the PBIS Team

**Figure 2.2**    Bronze PBIS Champion Model System—The ABCs to Success

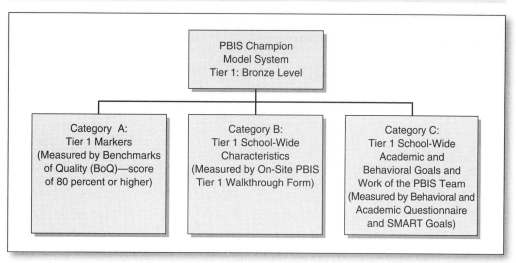

In the next four chapters, you will learn about each of the three categories and practical actions to build a strong Tier 1 foundation, assess the current state of your system, and read about lessons learned and stories from the field. Chapter 3 focuses on Category A and how to put in place ten critical PBIS markers. Chapter 4 concentrates on Category B, the four school-wide characteristics that must be solidly evident in order to build a strong Tier 1 foundation. Chapter 5 centers on Category C, the development of school-wide behavioral and academic goals, and the work of the PBIS team in support of those goals. Chapter 6 highlights lessons learned and case studies and also helps the reader bring it all together. Appendix Resources A includes the Bronze PBIS Champion Model System baseline assessments, Appendix Resources B includes the examples from the practical solutions sections in Chapters 3 and 4, and Appendix Resources C includes additional resources the authors believe to be helpful in implementing the Bronze PBIS Champion Model System.

# 3

# Getting Started With Category A— Tier 1 PBIS Markers

This chapter identifies and describes the Tier 1 markers of a Bronze PBIS Champion Model System, explains how to assess your system's current state relative to each marker, presents some challenges real schools faced and their approaches to addressing those challenges, and provides detailed lists of actions for moving a system from current state to desired future— Bronze PBIS Champion Model System. So what are the Tier 1 markers of a Bronze PBIS Champion Model System?

In order to build a strong Tier 1 PBIS foundation, ten critical markers must be in place:

- Marker 1: Establish and Operate an Effective PBIS Team
- Marker 2: Establish and Maintain Faculty/Staff Commitment
- Marker 3: Establish and Deploy Effective Procedures for Dealing With Discipline
- Marker 4: Establish a Data Entry Procedure and Design an Analysis Plan
- Marker 5: Establish a Set of School-Wide Behavior Expectations and Rules

- Marker 6: Establish a Behavior Reward/Recognition Program
- Marker 7: Develop and Deliver Lesson Plans for Teaching School-Wide Behavior Expectations and Rules
- Marker 8: Develop and Deploy a School-Wide PBIS Implementation Plan
- Marker 9: Establish Classroom Systems—Routines/Procedures
- Marker 10: Establish and Execute an Evaluation Plan

These markers can best be assessed through the Benchmarks of Quality (BoQ)—a tool used to help a school establish a Tier 1 PBIS implementation baseline and recognized as a valid tool to measure and monitor progress of PBIS implementation levels in schools (Cohen, Kincaid, & Childs, 2007). A complete Benchmarks of Quality (BoQ) Scoring Rubric (Adapted Version) can be found in Appendix A, A-1. The indicator evidencing a strong Tier 1 foundation in alignment with the Bronze PBIS Champion Model System is an overall BoQ score of 80 percent or higher, which is equivalent to 86 points or more out of a total 107 points.

We use the BoQ score as *one* of the measures for evidencing attainment of a Tier 1 Bronze PBIS Champion Model System. The first step toward developing a Tier 1 PBIS Bronze Champion Model System is to assess the current state of your own system using the BoQ tool. You will use the results of this survey to perform a gap analysis and get an understanding of where your system is in relation to the ten critical markers. It is important that honest responses are provided for all BoQ items because the information gained from the survey data is used to guide your next-step actions.

**Who should complete the BoQ?** In an effort to obtain accurate baseline information, a PBIS team should complete the survey. If you do not have a PBIS team established at the time of the baseline survey, the administrator of the school should complete the initial survey in collaboration with his or her school leadership team.

## TIER 1: THE TEN PBIS MARKERS

This section presents each of the ten Tier 1 PBIS markers, including the following details:

- Description of the marker
- Questions to consider in relation to the marker

- Assessing our current state: Where are we in relation to this marker?
- List of actions to advance the marker from current state to desired future and a reflection about next-step, high-leverage moves
- Cautions or red flags indicating that one or more areas of the marker may need to be addressed
- Examples from the field: challenges, practical solutions, and tools/resources used

## MARKER 1
## Establish and Operate an Effective PBIS Team

Assemble a PBIS team, five to seven diverse school staff members (e.g., representation from each grade level, department, or other influential members of the school staff such as custodian), who commit to meet at least one hour a month to assist and support PBIS implementation at a Champion Model level. An administrator is an active member of this team and guarantees that the team has time to meet. The PBIS team designates a person(s) as a PBIS coach or co-coaches of the team. The PBIS coach has the responsibility of ensuring that the PBIS team meets monthly and follows up on the commitments the team makes during monthly PBIS team meetings.

## QUESTIONS TO CONSIDER

- Does our school have a PBIS team? If yes, is our team operating effectively?
- Does the membership of our PBIS team broadly represent our system?
- Does our PBIS team have a written purpose or mission statement?
- Does our administrator actively support the PBIS team by attending all meetings as well as support the decisions and work of the team?
- Does our PBIS team meet monthly for approximately one hour?

## Assessing Our Current State:
## Where Are We in Relation to Marker 1?

| Marker 1: Establish and Operate an Effective PBIS Team | 3 points | 2 points | 1 point | 0 points | Score |
|---|---|---|---|---|---|
| 1. The PBIS team has administrative support. | Administrator(s) attended training, play an active role in the PBIS process, actively communicate their commitment, support the decisions of the PBIS team, and attend **all** team meetings. | Administrator(s) support the process, take as active a role as the rest of the PBIS team, and/or attend **most** meetings. | Administrator(s) support the process but don't take as active a role as the rest of the PBIS team, and/or attends **only a few** meetings. | Administrator(s) **do not** actively support the PBIS process. | ___/3 |
| 2. The PBIS team has regular meetings (at least monthly). | | The PBIS team meets monthly (**minimum of nine** one-hour meetings each school year). | The PBIS team meetings are not consistent (**five to eight**) monthly meetings each school year). | The PBIS team seldom meets (**fewer than five** monthly meetings during the school year). | ___/2 |
| 3. The PBIS team has established a clear mission/purpose. | | | The PBIS team **has** a written purpose/mission statement for the team (commonly completed on the cover sheet of the action plan). | There is **no** purpose/mission statement written for the PBIS team. | ___/1 |

*Source:* Childs, Kincaid, & George (2011). Used with permission.

Our school's overall score for Marker 1 (Establish and Operate an Effective PBIS Team) is ___/6.

*(Note: The overall score is calculated by adding points given for each rubric statement.)*

**ACTIONS TO ESTABLISH AND OPERATE AN EFFECTIVE PBIS TEAM**

- The administrator shares the research, purpose, and goals of PBIS and the role of the PBIS team with the entire staff and asks staff members to state their interest in being a member of the team.
- Administrator shows videos of a model PBIS school during staff trainings to encourage staff members to be part of the PBIS team (see Appendix A-2: PBIS Videos and School Visit Contact Information in Appendix Resources A).
- Assemble a PBIS team that includes five to seven diverse, positive, and influential members who commit to implementing PBIS at a Champion Model level. The administrator serves as an active member of the team.
- Calendar monthly sixty-minute PBIS team meetings for the entire school year during teacher's duty day, and the PBIS team adheres to the meeting schedule.
- The PBIS team members commit to establishing and following an agenda and norms for each meeting.
- The PBIS team creates a written purpose/mission statement focused on the criteria for operating at a PBIS Champion Model level.
- Select a PBIS coach (or co-coaches) from among PBIS team members. The PBIS coach helps facilitate meetings, monitors the work of the team by making sure that monthly meetings are held and follows up on commitments made by PBIS members during team meetings, researches fun ways to introduce PBIS to school staff, and provides ongoing communication to the staff.
- The PBIS team shares updates (ten to fifteen minutes) with the school staff at every staff or department meeting.

## OTHER ACTIONS TO CONSIDER

- Offer PBIS team membership as an adjunct duty or replacement for supervision duty.
- Ask a district office administrator to be a part of the school PBIS team.
- Establish a student PBIS team (may be part of a class or period). Assign a member of the adult PBIS team to serve as an adviser to the student PBIS team. The adviser meets monthly with the student PBIS team. Share monthly information from the student team with the adult PBIS team and then with all staff.
- For an alternative education setting, consider the entire staff as the PBIS team.

## CAUTION

If you find one or more of the following conditions or situations occurring at your school, view the condition/situation as a red flag that one or more areas of this marker—Establish and Operate an Effective PBIS Team—may need to be addressed.

### RED FLAGS

- The PBIS team has been established and meets for compliance reasons only.
- The PBIS team was thrown together and does not meet regularly to look at data.
- The administrator and PBIS team members are unclear as to what it takes to implement PBIS at a Champion Model level.
- Negative staff members or the teachers with the highest number of discipline referrals were selected to be a part of the PBIS team (although this will lead to important conversations for change, not suggested to have them as part of the team).
- The administrator does not or rarely attends PBIS meetings.
- The administrator does not support, as evidenced by his or her behaviors and actions, the decisions and work of the PBIS team.
- No evidence exists of an agenda, norms, and/or actions taken for each team meeting.
- PBIS meetings are cancelled due to other meetings taking priority.
- PBIS meetings are scheduled during nonduty times, and/or PBIS team members are assigned supervision duty or other responsibilities that conflict with PBIS meeting time and no coverage is provided.
- PBIS team meetings are not focused, and messaging to the entire staff about the work is not clear. (*The consequence is that team members begin to drop out of being a part of the team because the messaging to the entire school staff is not clear—therefore, reflecting on them in a negative light.*)
- The administrator and PBIS team cannot articulate the PBIS work and the purpose of why it is best for students.
- The administrator uses a top-down approach by telling staff what to do relative to PBIS without getting staff input.

Based on our assessment of current state for this marker and the suggested list of actions and red flags, what should our next move be?

_____

_____

_____

_____

_____

_____

_____

_____

_____

_____

≈◦≈

## FROM THE FIELD: MARKER 1—ESTABLISH AND OPERATE AN EFFECTIVE PBIS TEAM

**Challenge:** The PBIS team did not have an organized way to monitor PBIS team meetings, agenda items/outcomes, and follow-up on decisions made in PBIS team meetings. PBIS team meeting notes were not shared with the school staff.

**Practical Solution:** The PBIS team researched PBIS agendas that included documentation of the roles of all team members, required commitments, and addressed team meeting effectiveness. The team decided to use a structure called the PBIS Team Meeting Minutes and Problem-Solving Action Plan Form (Newton, Todd, Algozzine, Horner, & Algozzine, 2010). The PBIS team posts the meeting agenda on their school PBIS wall as well as e-mails an electronic copy to all members of the PBIS team and school staff. In addition to the principal who already receives a copy of the agenda as member of the PBIS team, the PBIS agenda is submitted to the district PBIS coordinator monthly to ensure that support and time is provided to meet the outcomes identified by the school team.

**Tool/Resource used:** PBIS Team Meeting Minutes and Problem-Solving Action Plan Form (see Appendix B-1 in Appendix Resources B)

**What is it?** A tool to assist PBIS teams in skillfully running problem-solving meetings and using data for decision making

## MARKER 2
## Establish and Maintain Faculty/Staff Commitment

Faculty/Staff commitment means that at least 80 percent of the school staff understands and supports PBIS implementation.

### QUESTIONS TO CONSIDER

- Are data regarding school-wide student behavior shared monthly with staff?
- Does our faculty/staff participate in establishing PBIS goals at least annually?
- Is our faculty/staff provided ongoing opportunities to provide feedback, offer suggestions, and make decisions regarding PBIS processes?
- Is faculty/staff approval sought for every PBIS process implemented, and are only the processes with majority staff approval implemented?

### Assessing Our Current State:
### Where Are We in Relation to Marker 2?

| Marker 2: Establish and Maintain Faculty/Staff Commitment | 3 points | 2 points | 1 point | 0 points | Score |
|---|---|---|---|---|---|
| 4. The faculty/staff members are aware of behavior problems across campus through regular data sharing. | | Data regarding school-wide behavior **are** shared with faculty/staff members monthly **(minimum of eight times** per year). | Data regarding school-wide behavior **are occasionally** shared with faculty/staff members **(three to seven times** per year). | Data **are not** regularly shared with faculty/staff members. Faculty/staff members may be given an update **zero to two times** per year. | ___/2 |
| 5. The faculty/staff members are involved in establishing and reviewing goals. | | **Most** faculty/staff members participate in establishing PBIS goals (i.e., surveys) on at least an annual basis. | **Some** of the faculty/staff members participate in establishing PBIS goals (i.e., surveys) on at least an annual basis. | The faculty/staff members **do not** participate in establishing PBIS goals. | ___/2 |

| Marker 2: Establish and Maintain Faculty/Staff Commitment | 3 points | 2 points | 1 point | 0 points | Score |
|---|---|---|---|---|---|
| 6. Faculty/staff feedback is obtained throughout year. | | The faculty/staff members **are given** opportunities to provide feedback, to offer suggestions, and to make choices in every step of the PBIS process (via staff surveys, voting process, suggestion box, etc.) Nothing is implemented without the majority of faculty/staff approval. | The faculty/staff members **are given some** opportunities to provide feedback, to offer suggestions, and to make some choices during the PBIS process. However, the team also makes decisions without input from faculty/staff members. | The faculty/staff members **are rarely given** the opportunity to participate in the PBIS process **(fewer than two times** per school year). | __/2 |

*Source:* Childs, Kincaid, & George (2011). Used with permission.

Our school's overall score for Marker 2 (Establish and Maintain Faculty/Staff Commitment) is __/6 points.

*(Note: The overall score is calculated by adding points given for each rubric statement.)*

---

## ACTIONS TO ESTABLISH AND MAINTAIN FACULTY/STAFF COMMITMENT

- Create the need for a PBIS system:
  - Provide school staff with an overview of the research that supports PBIS implementation.
  - Share behavior data of the school, and have staff identify areas of need.
  - Explain and demonstrate to staff how a strong Tier 1 PBIS system will support the school to more effectively use resources for students most in need of behavior interventions and increase staff support with discipline challenges.
  - Enlist a teacher or influential PBIS team member to share reasons why PBIS is necessary.

*(Continued)*

(Continued)

- Show videos of what effective PBIS implementation looks like in schools and/or take staff to visit a model PBIS school (see Appendix A-2: PBIS Video List and School Visit Contact Information in Appendix Resources A).
- Share with staff a school-wide behavior goal of a school operating at Bronze PBIS Champion Model level and the criteria to achieve at this level (see Chapter 5).
- Create ongoing opportunities for faculty to provide feedback, offer suggestions, and make decisions regarding PBIS processes. Create a method for staff to provide ongoing input to the PBIS team regarding PBIS implementation, such as an input board located in a specific room in the school.
- Seek staff approval for every PBIS process, and implement only the processes with critical mass (about 75 to 80 percent) staff approval.
- Share school-wide student behavior data with staff at least monthly.
- Include a meeting outcome and agenda item related to PBIS system operations on every staff and department meeting agenda.
- Clearly communicate and message all PBIS information.
- Provide clear and timely communication on how office-managed behaviors are handled by the administration.
- Review PBIS goals (academic and behavioral) with staff at least annually, and provide opportunity for input and feedback regarding the goals based on relevant data.

## OTHER ACTIONS TO CONSIDER

- Share behavior data, PBIS videos, and samples of PBIS model systems that are grade-level appropriate (elementary school, middle school, high school, and alternative education) for your school setting.
- Select, with input from staff, a student PBIS team who monthly provides input and feedback to the adult PBIS team regarding PBIS implementation.
- Elicit student feedback regarding the top three perceived problems at the school and the challenges associated with these problems, and then share this information with the staff.

## CAUTION

If you find one or more of the following conditions or situations occurring at your school, view the condition or situation as a red flag that one or more areas of this marker—Establish and Maintain Faculty Commitment—may need to be addressed.

## RED FLAGS

- The message sent to faculty, students, and the community is that PBIS implementation replaces discipline.
- Once school-wide expectations are taught in each setting, adults abdicate responsibility for reinforcing appropriate behaviors and correcting inappropriate behaviors.
- Faculty is directed to implement PBIS but has not been educated about what that entails.
- Faculty input and feedback about PBIS implementation and goal setting is not collected and/or used.
- PBIS team members serve for compliance reasons only and **do not** operationalize the belief that PBIS will help improve their school system or optimize its use as an improvement strategy.
- PBIS is not a topic at every faculty meeting, and administration is the only one who shares information about PBIS.
- Every school initiative (academic and behavioral) is not connected with PBIS.

Based on our assessment of current state for this marker and the suggested list of actions and red flags, what should our next move be?

_____

_____

_____

_____

_____

_____

_____

_____

_____

_____

## FROM THE FIELD: MARKER 2—ESTABLISH AND MAINTAIN FACULTY/STAFF COMMITMENT

**Challenge:** The PBIS team needed a way to get students and staff involved in learning the school-wide behavior expectations and rules in multiple settings.

**Practical Solution:** The PBIS team developed a two-day teaching and learning event called Passport to Learning—School-Wide Behavior Expectations. During two designated days, staff members were expected to teach students the school-wide behavior expectations in multiple settings. A script was developed to support staff in teaching these expectations. Teachers were expected to educate students on the expectations in their own classrooms prior to students advancing to the rest of the settings. Teachers and other support staff (e.g., librarian taught expectations in the library setting using the script) demonstrated non-examples of the expected behaviors (inappropriate behaviors) and volunteers or selected students demonstrated examples of the expected behaviors (appropriate behaviors) for each identified setting. Each student was given a passport that indicated each location or setting. Students rotated to the various settings, and once they learned the expectation for a given setting, their passports to learning were stamped.

**Tool/Resource used:** Teacher Behavior Day Script and Passport (see Appendix B-2 in Appendix Resources B)

**What is it?** The Teacher Behavior Day Script is a script that guides staff in teaching the school-wide behavior expectations in each designated setting. This script supports staff and students in developing knowledge of what the expected behaviors look like and sound like in each setting (examples and non-examples are provided for staff and student demonstrations).

The Passport is a travel document that students have stamped as they evidence learning of the behavior expectations and rules in each location or setting.

### MARKER 3
### Establish and Deploy Effective Procedures for Dealing With Discipline

Discipline procedures include both minor and major discipline incidents, both *inside* and *outside* the classroom. Discipline procedures should be clearly defined, communicated, and understood by all staff. All staff members should clearly understand the difference between what constitutes a minor and major discipline incident, be able to clearly articulate the procedure for a given discipline incident, and consistently follow or implement the procedures.

## QUESTIONS TO CONSIDER

- Has our PBIS team established clear, written procedures that lay out the process for handling both major and minor discipline incidents? Do our procedures also include crisis situations?
- Does a procedure exist in our system to document and track (i.e., a form, database entry, file in room) both major and minor behavior incidents?
- Do our referral forms include information that is useful in decision making? Do our referral forms request ALL of the following information: student's name, date, time of incident, grade level, referring staff, location of incident, gender, problem behavior, possible motivation, others involved, and administrative decision?
- Does written documentation exist in our system that includes all problem behaviors and clear definitions of those problem behaviors?
- Are all staff members clear about which behaviors or incidents are identified as minor or major?
- Are all staff members clear about which behaviors are staff managed and which are sent to the office (appropriate use of office referrals)?
- What are our system's predetermined appropriate responses to major behavior problems?
- Does evidence exist that all staff members are aware of and use an array of our predetermined appropriate responses to major behavior problems?

### Assessing Our Current State: Where Are We in Relation to Marker 3?

| Marker 3: Establish and Deploy Effective Procedures for Dealing With Discipline | 3 points | 2 points | 1 point | 0 points | Score |
|---|---|---|---|---|---|
| 7. The discipline process is described in narrative format or depicted in graphic format. | | The PBIS team **has** established clear, written procedures that lay out the process for handling both major and minor discipline incidents (**includes** crisis situations). | The PBIS team **has** established clear, written procedures that lay out the process for handling both major and minor discipline incidents (**does not include** crisis situations). | The PBIS team **has not** established clear, written procedures for discipline incidents and/or there is no differentiation between major and minor incidents. | __/2 |

*(Continued)*

(Continued)

| Marker 3: Establish and Deploy Effective Procedures for Dealing With Discipline | 3 points | 2 points | 1 point | 0 points | Score |
|---|---|---|---|---|---|
| 8. The discipline process includes documentation procedures. | | | **A procedure exists** to document and track both major and minor behavior incidents (i.e., form, database entry, file in room, etc.). | **No procedure exists** to document and track major and minor behavior incidents (i.e., form, database entry, file in room, etc.). | ___/1 |
| 9. The discipline referral form includes information useful in decision making. | | Information on the referral form includes **all** of the required fields: Student's name, date, time of incident, grade level, referring staff, location of incident, gender, problem behavior, possible motivation, others involved, and administrative decision. | The referral form includes **all** of the required fields, but also includes unnecessary information that is not used to make decisions and may cause confusion. | The referral form **lacks** one or more of the required fields **or does not** exist. | ___/2 |
| 10. The problem behaviors are defined. | Written documentation exists that includes clear definitions of **all** behaviors listed. | **All** of the behaviors are defined **but some** of the definitions are unclear. | **Not all** behaviors are defined or **some** definitions are unclear. | **No** written documentation of definitions exists. | ___/3 |
| 11. The major/minor behaviors are clearly differentiated. | | **Most** faculty/staff members are clear about which behaviors are staff managed and which are sent to the office (i.e., appropriate use of office referrals). Those behaviors are clearly defined, differentiated, and documented. | **Some** staff members are unclear about which behaviors are staff managed and which are sent to the office (i.e., appropriate use of office referrals) or no documentation exists. | Specific major/minor behaviors **are not** clearly defined, differentiated or documented. | ___/2 |

| Marker 3: Establish and Deploy Effective Procedures for Dealing With Discipline | 3 points | 2 points | 1 point | 0 points | Score |
|---|---|---|---|---|---|
| 12. **There is a suggested array of appropriate responses to major (office-managed) problem behaviors.** | | | There is evidence that **all** administrative staff members are aware of and use an array of predetermined appropriate responses to major behavior problems. | There is evidence that **some** administrative staff members are not aware of, or do not follow, an array of predetermined appropriate responses to major behavior problems. | ___/1 |

*Source:* Childs, Kincaid, & George (2011). Used with permission.

Our school's overall score for Marker 3 (Establish and Deploy Effective Procedures for Dealing with Discipline) is ___/11 points.

*(Note: The overall score is calculated by adding points given for each rubric statement.)*

---

### ACTIONS TO ESTABLISH AND DEPLOY EFFECTIVE PROCEDURES FOR DEALING WITH DISCIPLINE

- The PBIS team identifies what constitutes minor and major behaviors/incidents in the system, clearly defines all behaviors/incidents, and documents them in writing. The team gets input and feedback from staff during this process.
- The PBIS team establishes clear, written procedures that lay out the process for handling both major and minor discipline incidents including crisis situations. The team gets input and feedback from staff during this process.
- The PBIS team creates a draft flowchart regarding procedures on handling minor and major behaviors in and out of the classroom and shares the flowchart with staff for feedback. The team finalizes the flowchart based on feedback.
- The PBIS team decides which behaviors are staff managed and which are sent to the office (appropriate use of office referrals) and clearly defines and differentiates those behaviors in writing. The team gets input and feedback from staff during this process.
- Inventory your school referral form for the information necessary to make useful decisions: student's name, date, time of incident, grade level, referring

*(Continued)*

(Continued)

staff, location of incident, gender, problem behavior, possible motivation, others involved, and administrative decision. Make revisions to the referral form as appropriate. *(Note: Definitions for minor and major behaviors should align with office discipline referral form and the flowchart for how behavior is handled.)*

- Educate staff on (a) the difference between minor and major incidents, (b) classroom-managed and office-managed discipline, and (c) documenting and tracking procedures. Provide staff members time to practice how they would handle major and minor discipline incidents.
- Identify and educate staff on a variety of predetermined appropriate responses to minor and major behavior problems.
- Provide refreshers on the discipline procedures during staff meetings throughout the school year.

## OTHER ACTIONS TO CONSIDER

- Set up a pilot group of teachers to field-test proposed procedures and forms (paper forms or electronic version of forms) prior to all school-wide deployment, and identify strengths of the processes and forms and areas for possible improvement. Make necessary adjustments as appropriate before implementing them school-wide.
- Use pilot groups to share procedures with the rest of the staff, and help train staff on implementation.
- Provide teachers with classroom-managed discipline options (provide opportunities for staff members to share with each other during staff meetings effective processes for classroom management).
- Enlarge (poster size) the discipline flowchart and the office discipline referral, and structure opportunities for staff to practice using the flowchart and filling out referrals given various scenarios.
- For secondary systems, create a process with the PBIS team to collect minor and major behavior data from each class period and in all settings (process of tracking how many referrals in each period overall).
- Seek input from influential staff members on ways to improve teacher support with discipline.

## CAUTION

If you find one or more of the following conditions or situations occurring at your school, view the condition or situation as a red flag that one or more areas of this marker—Establish and Deploy Effective Procedures for Dealing with Discipline—may need to be addressed.

| RED FLAGS |
|---|
| • The staff is unable to articulate the reasons why it is important to have clear and consistent processes for discipline.<br>• The staff has not been trained on the discipline procedures of the school.<br>• School discipline data are never or rarely used to demonstrate the need for improvement and consistency in a given area.<br>• Teachers are not provided with options for classroom-managed discipline consequences/interventions.<br>• Administration does not follow through on discipline or does not communicate with staff in a timely manner about the discipline consequences administered.<br>• No system exists to train new staff members on how to use the discipline procedures (no system for new staff entry to the school). |

Based on our assessment of current state for this marker and the suggested list of actions and red flags, what should our next move be?

_____

_____

_____

_____

_____

_____

_____

_____

_____

_____

## FROM THE FIELD: MARKER 3—ESTABLISH AND DEPLOY EFFECTIVE PROCEDURES FOR DEALING WITH DISCIPLINE

**Challenge:** The PBIS school team was given the task of organizing the minor and major behavior school discipline procedures including procedures for collecting behavior data both inside and outside the classroom. The school staff members indicated that they did not know the process for handling and documenting behavior in the different settings. They also told the administration that they were not clear on the difference between minor and major behaviors, which resulted in the collection of inaccurate behavior data because there was not a common interpretation or understanding of type of behavior incident.

**Practical Solution:** The PBIS school team worked with the school administrative team to develop a list of minor and major behaviors. The team elicited feedback from the staff members during a staff meeting on whether or not the behaviors they had listed in the minor and major categories seemed accurate. The PBIS team took the feedback from the staff to their next PBIS team meeting and drafted flowcharts detailing steps for documenting minor and major behavior incidents, in and out of the classroom. The school staff reviewed the flowcharts at the beginning of the school year during a staff meeting. Staff members were provided the opportunity to practice the steps in the flowchart and ask clarifying questions. A PBIS team member/administrator trains yard duty staff and new school staff on the behavior flowcharts during their orientation to the school.

**Tool/Resource used:** Minor and Major Behavior Data Tracking Flowcharts (see Appendix B-3 in Appendix Resources B)

**What is it?** The Minor and Major Behavior Data Tracking Flowcharts are visual pictures that show all the steps in the process for collecting and entering behavior data. The four flowcharts depict the data collection and entry processes for minor incidents inside the classroom, minor incidents outside the classroom, major incidents inside the classroom, and major incidents outside the classroom.

> **MARKER 4**
> **Establish a Data Entry Procedure and**
> **Design an Analysis Plan**

The PBIS team establishes a data entry procedure and designs an analysis plan to ensure that accurate and up-to-date data are analyzed, communicated to, and understood by the entire staff. A data entry procedure is a process of inputting behavior data into an information management system equipped with the capabilities to produce behavior reports, graphs, and charts for the PBIS team to use for problem solving and decision making. A data analysis plan is designed to help monitor progress toward meeting PBIS goals and inform the system about the effectiveness of PBIS implementation/processes.

## QUESTIONS TO CONSIDER

- Does our school have an information or data management system that collects and analyzes office discipline referral data?
- Can our school's data management system quickly output data in graph format?
- Does our school's information or data management system allow our PBIS team members access to ALL of the following information: average referrals per day per month, by location, by problem behavior, by time of day, by student, as well as provide us the capability to compare between years?
- Does our school's information or data management system also collect and store data other than discipline data such as attendance, grades, faculty attendance, and survey data? Does our school-wide PBIS team use this data to help determine progress and successes?
- Does one of our PBIS team members, at least monthly, organize data into a graph format or other easily understood format and provide this data in printed form to the PBIS team for analysis and decision making?
- Does our PBIS team analyze data at least monthly to determine progress, next steps, and successes?
- Is data shared with our PBIS team and faculty at least monthly?

## Assessing Our Current State:
## Where Are We in Relation to Marker 4?

| Marker 4: Establish a Data Entry Procedure and Design an Analysis Plan | 3 points | 2 points | 1 point | 0 points | Score |
|---|---|---|---|---|---|
| **13. The data system is used to collect and analyze office discipline referral data.** | The database can quickly output data in graph format and allows the team access to **all** of the following information: average referrals per day per month, by location, by problem behavior, by time of day, by student, and compare between years. | **All** of the information can be obtained from the database (average referrals per day per month, by location, by problem behavior, by time of day, by student, and compare between years), **though it may not be** in graph format, may require more faculty/staff time to pull the information, or require faculty/staff time to make sense of the data. | Only **partial** information can be obtained (lacking either the number of average referrals per day per month, location, problem behavior, time of day, student, and compare patterns between years). | The data system is **not able** to provide any of the necessary information the team needs to make school-wide decisions. | ___/3 |
| **14. Additional data are collected (i.e., attendance, grades, faculty/staff attendance, surveys) and used by the school-wide PBIS team.** | | | The PBIS team collects and considers data other than discipline data to help determine progress and successes (i.e., attendance, grades, faculty/staff attendance, school surveys, etc.). | The PBIS team does **not** collect or consider data other than discipline data to help determine progress and successes (i.e., attendance, grades, faculty/staff attendance, school surveys, etc.). | ___/1 |
| **15. Data are analyzed by team at least monthly.** | | Data **are** printed, analyzed, and put into graph format or other easy-to-understand format by a member of the PBIS team **monthly** (minimum). | Data **are** printed, analyzed, and put into graph format or other easy-to-understand format by a team member **less than once a month**. | Data are **not** analyzed. | ___/2 |

| Marker 4: Establish a Data Entry Procedure and Design an Analysis Plan | 3 points | 2 points | 1 point | 0 points | Score |
|---|---|---|---|---|---|
| 16. Data are shared with team and faculty/staff monthly (minimum). | | Data are shared with the PBIS team and faculty/staff **at least once a month**. | Data are shared with the PBIS team and faculty/staff **less than one time per month**. | Data **are not** reviewed by the PBIS team and shared with faculty/staff. | ___/2 |

*Source:* Childs, Kincaid, & George (2011). Used with permission.

Our school's overall score for Marker 4 (Establish a Data Entry Procedure and Design an Analysis Plan) is ___/8 points.

*(Note: The overall score is calculated by adding points given for each rubric statement.)*

---

### ACTIONS TO ESTABLISH A DATA ENTRY PROCEDURE AND DESIGN AN ANALYSIS PLAN

- Inventory the database of your school's information management system for the following information: average referrals per day per month, by location, by problem behavior, by time of day, by student, as well as for its capability to compare data between years. If any of the information does not exist in the system, establish a database with this information. Check on the capability of the database to quickly output data in graph format. If capability does not exist, modify the system.
- The PBIS team identifies the types of reports available through the school's information management system that would be valuable to analyze and use regarding school discipline and attendance data.
- Designate one member of the PBIS team to monitor data entry to make sure that the data are current and brought to every monthly PBIS team meeting.
- The PBIS team provides a monthly recap of the data analyzed to the entire staff via e-mail or hard copy.
- Establish a procedure to correct inaccurate data entry.
- During staff meetings, review behavior data and discuss any procedural challenges to data entry. Provide staff refreshers on accurate data entry procedures.
- Post behavior data and other information on a staff PBIS wall for staff reference.
- The PBIS team provides staff with data regarding PBIS implementation and progress toward achieving PBIS goals.

## OTHER ACTIONS TO CONSIDER

- Elicit staff feedback on the easiest way to gather behavior data for analysis.
- Provide a staff member supervision coverage or a stipend to help organize, print, and disseminate behavior data for monthly PBIS meetings.

## CAUTION

If you find one or more of the following conditions or situations occurring at your school, view the condition or situation as a red flag that one or more areas of this marker—Establish a Data Entry Procedure and Design an Analysis Plan—may need to be addressed.

### RED FLAGS

- Behavior data are never or rarely discussed at staff meetings.
- Staff is unable to articulate the reasons why it is important to fill out and turn in referral forms in a timely manner.
- Staff has never been trained on how to analyze behavior data (charts, graphs, etc.).
- School behavior data are inconsistently entered into the system, therefore skewing the data output (charts, graphs, etc.).
- Teachers feel like they will be penalized if they turn in referral forms.
- The administration does not provide a staff member time to ensure that the behavior data are entered into the data system in a timely manner.

❧❧❧

Based on our assessment of current state for this marker and the suggested list of actions and red flags, what should our next move be?

_____

_____

_____

_____

_____

_____

_____

_____

_____

_____

ಧಿ ಧಿ

## FROM THE FIELD: MARKER 4—
## ESTABLISH A DATA ENTRY PROCEDURE
## AND DESIGN AN ANALYSIS PLAN

**Challenge:** The behavior data at School B were not shared or analyzed with staff. The staff was unaware of behavior trends or hot spots (highs discipline areas) in the school. Feedback about behavior was not obtained from staff.

**Practical Solution:** The PBIS team used an electronic communication method to share behavior information with school staff. Following monthly PBIS meetings, the administrator or PBIS coach sends to all staff members an e-mail indicating behavior data findings and highlighting the area for focus.

**Tool/Resource used:** Behavior Snapshot E-Mail Example (see Appendix B-4 in Appendix Resources B)

**What is it?** Electronic communication method (e-mail) used to provide consistent and timely behavior data and information to the staff. It is a quick snapshot of behavior data findings (graph format) and highlights areas for focus. This communication method also provides the opportunity and structure for staff to communicate back with prevention and intervention ideas, and staff members are encouraged to do so.

**MARKER 5**
**Establish a Set of School-Wide**
**Behavior Expectations and Rules**

The PBIS team, with the input of staff, establishes a set of positively stated school-wide behavior expectations and rules for students and staff in all settings (classroom, bathroom, hallway, computer lab, bus stop, cafeteria, library, office, gym, etc.). The set of school-wide behavior expectations is three to five positively stated behavior expectations that apply to all students and staff in the school and in all school settings. Rules are the positively stated guidelines or a rubric of what the expectations look like in each setting (i.e., positively stated = raise hand and wait for your turn to speak; negatively stated = no blurting out).

## QUESTIONS TO CONSIDER

- Does our school have a set of three to five positively stated school-wide behavior expectations? If yes, are our school-wide expectations visibly posted around the school in classrooms and at least three other settings such as the hallways, cafeteria, and the school office?
- Do our school-wide expectations apply to both students and staff? Do students and staff clearly understand our school-wide expectations, and does everyone understand that these expectations apply to all of us?
- Does our school develop rules for specific settings (classroom and other settings where data suggest rules are needed), and are these rules posted in all the most problematic areas of our school?
- Are our rules linked to our school-wide expectations?
- Was most of our staff involved in providing feedback or input into the development of school-wide expectations and rules?

### Assessing Our Current State:
### Where Are We in Relation to Marker 5?

| Marker 5: Establish a Set of School-Wide Behavior Expectations and Rules | 3 points | 2 points | 1 point | 0 points | Score |
|---|---|---|---|---|---|
| 17. **Three to five positively stated** | **Three to five** positively stated school-wide behavior | **Three to five** positively stated behavior expectations | **Three to five** positively stated behavior expectations **are** | Behavior expectations **are not** posted | __/3 |

| Marker 5: Establish a Set of School-Wide Behavior Expectations and Rules | 3 points | 2 points | 1 point | 0 points | Score |
|---|---|---|---|---|---|
| **school-wide behavior expectations are posted around school.** | expectations are visibly posted around the school. Areas posted include the classroom and a minimum of three other school settings (i.e., cafeteria, hallway, front office, etc.). | are visibly posted in **most** important areas (i.e., classroom, cafeteria, hallway), but one area may be missed. | **not** clearly visible in common areas. | or there are too few or too many behavior expectations. | |
| 18. **Behavior expectations apply to both students and faculty/staff members.** | PBIS team **has** communicated that behavior expectations apply to **all students and all faculty/staff members.** | The PBIS team **has** behavior expectations that apply to **all students and all faculty/staff members but haven't** specifically communicated that they apply to faculty/staff as well as students. | Behavior expectations refer **only** to student behavior. | There are **no** behavior expectations. | ___/3 |
| 19. **Rules are developed and posted for specific settings (settings where data suggested rules are needed).** | | Rules are posted in **all** of the most problematic areas in the school. | Rules are posted in **some but not all** of the most problematic areas of the school. | Rules **are not** posted in any of the most problematic areas of the school. | ___/2 |
| 20. **Rules are linked to behavior expectations.** | | | When taught or enforced, faculty/staff members **consistently** link the rules with the school-wide behavior expectations. | When taught or enforced, faculty/staff members **do not consistently** link the rules with the school-wide behavior expectations and/or rules are taught or enforced separately from behavior expectations. | ___/1 |

(Continued)

| Marker 5: Establish a Set of School-Wide Behavior Expectations and Rules | 3 points | 2 points | 1 point | 0 points | Score |
|---|---|---|---|---|---|
| 21. **Faculty/staff members are involved in development of behavior expectations and rules.** | | **Most** faculty/staff members were involved in providing feedback/input into the development of the school-wide behavior expectations and rules (i.e., survey, feedback, initial brainstorming session, election process, etc.). | **Some** faculty/staff members were involved in providing feedback/input into the development of the school-wide behavior expectations and rules. | Faculty/staff members **were not** involved in providing feedback/input into the development of the school-wide behavior expectations and rules. | __/2 |

*Source:* Childs, Kincaid, & George (2011). Used with permission.

Our school's overall score for Marker 5 (Establish a Set of School-Wide Behavior Expectations and Rules) is __/11 points.

*(Note: The overall score is calculated by adding points given for each rubric statement.)*

---

### ACTIONS TO ESTABLISH A SET OF SCHOOL-WIDE BEHAVIOR EXPECTATIONS AND RULES

- The PBIS team in collaboration with administration develops three to four sets of school-wide behavior expectations to present to staff. Tips: Make the expectations short and easy to remember. Try to tie the set of expectations to something that students and staff will remember—for example, CLAWS (Come Prepared, Live Responsibly, Act Safely, Work Together, and Show Respect) (bear mascot). Identify a signal or nonverbal representation—for example, Strive for Five, an open hand of five fingers wherein each finger represents a school-wide behavior expectation. Facilitate a process with all staff members to make a decision on a set of school-wide behavior expectations—critical mass support (at least 75 to 80 percent of staff).
- The PBIS team gets input from stakeholders in each setting to help formulate, on average, three to six rules for each setting (e.g., the librarian is asked

for feedback on what the school-wide expectation of respect looks like in the library—to help establish the rules for this setting).

- The PBIS team reviews the rules developed by the stakeholders to make sure that all rules are positively stated and that each rule can be taught to the students (e.g., if the rule is to walk quietly in the hallway, students can be shown the wrong way [non-example] and right way [example] to walk quietly in the hallway).
- The PBIS team creates a behavior grid that includes all the school-wide behavior expectations and rules of the school (see Appendix A-3: Behavior Grid in Appendix Resources A).

## OTHER ACTIONS TO CONSIDER

- Gather input from students and departments on what the school-wide behavior expectations and rules should be.
- The PBIS team quizzes staff on school-wide behavior expectations during staff meetings.

## CAUTION

If you find one or more of the following conditions or situations occurring at your school, view the condition or situation as a red flag that one or more areas of this marker—Establish a Set of School-Wide Behavior Expectations and Rules—may need to be addressed.

### RED FLAGS

- Staff was not given an opportunity to provide input or feedback on the development of the school-wide behavior expectations and rules.
- Staff is not educated on the importance of creating consistent and clear school-wide behavior expectations and rules.
- Consistent language is not used to discuss school-wide behavior expectations and rules.
- Expectations and rules are negatively stated (e.g., no talking, no screaming).
- Visuals of school-wide behavior expectations and rules are posted but never or rarely referenced.

❧❧

Based on our assessment of current state for this marker and the suggested list of actions and red flags, what should our next move be?

_____

_____

_____

_____

_____

_____

_____

_____

_____

❧❧

## FROM THE FIELD: MARKER 5—ESTABLISH A SET OF SCHOOL-WIDE BEHAVIOR EXPECTATIONS AND RULES

**Challenge:** A PBIS team at a middle school needed a method for collecting input from students on appropriate rules in each school setting (i.e., bathroom, quad area, gym, office) that aligned with the school-wide behavior expectations.

**Practical Solution:** The PBIS team created a blank grid that included all of settings with an area to describe inappropriate demonstrations (non-examples) and appropriate demonstrations (examples) for each school-wide behavior expectation. Four classrooms were randomly selected (two seventh grade and two eighth grade) to gather input from students on what their opinions were on what appropriate rules should be in each setting. The PBIS team took the student input and shared it with the staff at a staff meeting. The PBIS team used a similar method with the staff members to elicit their input before drafting a template of all the rules for each setting aligned with the school-wide behavior expectation. The template reflected student and staff input.

**Tool/Resource used:** Student Input Form—Establishing Rules for Each Setting (see Appendix B-5 in Appendix Resources B)

**What is it?** A form designed to quickly gather student input regarding what appropriate behaviors look like in each setting aligned to the school-wide behavior expectations. This tool helped the PBIS team develop school rules in various settings aligned with the school-wide expectations.

---

### MARKER 6
### Establish a Behavior Reward/Recognition Program

Establish a system that rewards and recognizes students and staff for making progress toward and ongoing demonstration of school-wide behavior expectations.

---

## QUESTIONS TO CONSIDER

- Does our school have a system of rewards to recognize students and staff for progress toward and ongoing demonstration of school-wide behavior expectations, and is the system implemented consistently across campus?
- Does our school use a variety of methods to reward students?
- Does our school provide rewards for behaviors that are identified in our school-wide expectations and rules, and does staff verbalize the appropriate behavior when giving a reward?
- Does our school vary rewards throughout the year, and do the rewards reflect student interests (considerations given to student age, culture, gender, and ability level to maintain student interest)?
- Does our school have a high ratio of teacher reinforcement of appropriate behavior to correction of inappropriate behavior such as 4:1 (4 positives to 1 negative)?
- Does our school involve students in identifying and developing incentives/rewards?
- Does our system include incentives for staff, and are these incentives delivered consistently?

## Assessing Our Current State:
## Where Are We in Relation to Marker 6?

| Marker 6: Establish a Behavior Reward/ Recognition Program | 3 points | 2 points | 1 point | 0 points | Score |
|---|---|---|---|---|---|
| 22. **A system of rewards has elements that are implemented consistently across campus.** | The reward system guidelines and procedures **are** implemented consistently across campus. Almost all members of the school are participating appropriately (**at least 90 percent** participation). | The reward system guidelines and procedures **are** implemented consistently across campus. However, some faculty/staff members choose not to participate or participation does not meet the established criteria (**at least 75 percent** participation). | The reward system guidelines and procedures **are not** implemented consistently because several faculty/staff members choose not to participate or participation does not meet the established criteria (**at least 50 percent** participation). | There is no identifiable reward system or a large percentage of faculty/staff members are not participating (**less than 50 percent** participation). | ___/3 |
| 23. **A variety of methods are used to reward students.** | | The school **uses** a variety of methods to reward students (i.e., cashing in tokens/points). There should be opportunities that include tangible items, praise/ recognition, and social activities/ events. Students with few/many tokens/points have equal opportunities to cash them in for rewards. However, larger rewards are given to those earning more tokens/points. | The school **uses** a variety of methods to reward students, **but** students do not have access to a variety of rewards in a consistent and timely manner. | The school **uses only one** set method to reward students (i.e., tangibles only) or there are no opportunities for children to cash in tokens or select rewards. Only students who meet the quotas actually get rewarded; students with fewer tokens cannot cash in tokens for a smaller reward. | ___/2 |
| 24. **Rewards are linked to behavior expectations and rules.** | Rewards are provided for behaviors that **are** linked to the behavior | Rewards are provided for behaviors that **are** linked to the behavior | Rewards are provided for behaviors that **are** linked to the behavior | Rewards **are** provided for behaviors that **are not** linked to the behavior | ___/3 |

| Marker 6: Establish a Behavior Reward/ Recognition Program | 3 points | 2 points | 1 point | 0 points | Score |
|---|---|---|---|---|---|
| | expectations/ rules and faculty/ staff members **verbalize** the appropriate behavior when giving rewards. | expectations/ rules and faculty/ staff members **sometimes verbalize** appropriate behaviors when giving rewards. | expectations/ rules but faculty/ staff members **rarely** verbalize appropriate behaviors when giving rewards. | expectations/ rules. | |
| 25. **Rewards are varied to maintain student interest.** | | The rewards are varied throughout the year and **reflect** students' interests (i.e., consider the student age, culture, gender, and ability level to maintain student interest). | The rewards are varied throughout the school year but **may not** reflect students' interests. | The rewards **are not** varied throughout the school year and **do not** reflect students' interests. | ___/2 |
| 26. **The ratio of acknowledgement to corrections is high.** | The ratio of teacher reinforcement of appropriate behavior to correction of inappropriate behavior is **high** (i.e., 4:1). | The ratio of teacher reinforcement of appropriate behavior to correction of inappropriate behavior is **moderate** (i.e., 2:1). | The ratio of teacher reinforcement of appropriate behavior to correction of inappropriate behavior is **about the same** (i.e., 1:1). | The ratio of teacher reinforcement of appropriate behavior to correction of inappropriate behavior is **low** (i.e., 1:4). | ___/3 |
| 27. **The students are involved in identifying/ developing incentives.** | | | The students **are often** involved in identifying/ developing incentives. | The students **are rarely** involved in identifying/ developing incentives. | ___/1 |
| 28. **The system includes incentives for faculty/staff members.** | | The system **includes** incentives for faculty/staff members and they **are** delivered consistently. | The system **includes** incentives for faculty/staff members, but they **are not** delivered consistently. | The system **does not** include incentives for faculty/staff members. | ___/2 |

*Source:* Childs, Kincaid, & George (2011). Used with permission.

Our school's overall score for Marker 6 (Establish a Behavior Reward/Recognition Program) is ___/16 points.

*(Note: The overall score is calculated by adding points given for each rubric statement.)*

## ACTIONS TO ESTABLISH A
## BEHAVIOR REWARD/RECOGNITION PROGRAM

- The PBIS team develops, with input from staff and students, a school-wide recognition system aligned with the school-wide behavior expectations. The system should recognize individuals and groups (classroom/staff).
- The PBIS team and administration develops a calendar for recognizing students and staff.
- The PBIS team and administration communicate the school-wide recognition system to all stakeholders (i.e., students, staff, and community).
- Designate an individual (administrator or PBIS coach) to monitor that the reward/recognition system is executed on a weekly, quarterly, or by semester basis.
- The PBIS team provides refreshers to the staff on how to use and apply the reward/recognition program consistently.
- Administration works in collaboration with the PBIS team to message to all staff through various communication methods (staff meetings, e-mail, etc.) the importance of using positive language and specific verbal recognition (praise for demonstrating specific expected behaviors). Reinforce appropriate behavior to correction of inappropriate behavior at a high ratio—4:1.

## OTHER ACTIONS TO CONSIDER

- Involve students in weekly announcements that include information about the reward/recognition system and recognizes individuals and groups for appropriate behavior.
- Ask for donations from the community to support the reward/recognition program.
- Survey students on new ideas for incentives.

## CAUTION

If you find one or more of the following conditions or situations occurring at your school, view the condition or situation as a red flag that one or more areas of this marker—Establish a Behavior Reward/Recognition Program—may need to be addressed.

### RED FLAGS

- Staff are not educated on how to effectively use the recognition program.
- Students and staff are inconsistently rewarded.
- The reward/recognition system is not aligned to school-wide behavior expectations and rules.

- Administration is not involved in the rewards/recognition process.
- Reward/recognition system is so complicated that it is too difficult to implement and monitor.
- No person (administrator or PBIS coach) has been designated to ensure that the reward/recognition system is executed on a weekly basis.
- The PBIS team does not revisit monthly the reward/recognition system for effectiveness.
- Incentives or rewards do not reflect the interests or requests of the stakeholders.

---

Based on our assessment of current state for this marker and the suggested list of actions and red flags, what should our next move be?

_____

_____

_____

_____

_____

_____

_____

_____

_____

_____

_____

---

## FROM THE FIELD: MARKER 6—ESTABLISH A BEHAVIOR REWARD/RECOGNITION PROGRAM

**Challenge:** The PBIS team needed a method to communicate the behavior reward/recognition system to all students and staff. The school's history of recognizing students and staff was inconsistently applied, and students and staff lost interest and ownership in the system. The prior reward/recognition system had not been aligned with behavior expectations of the school.

**Practical Solution:** The PBIS team created a section insert for the Student/Parent Handbook and the Faculty Handbook detailing the school-wide behavior reward/recognition system. The reward/recognition system was aligned with school-wide behavior expectations. A copy of the handbook was provided to every staff member and parent connected to the school.

**Tool/Resource used:** Behavior Reward/Recognition Program Insert to Student/Parent Handbook and Faculty Handbook (see Appendix B-6 in Appendix Resources B)

**What is it?** A sample handbook insert detailing all aspects of the school-wide behavior reward/recognition system that is inserted into the Student/Parent Handbook and the Faculty Handbook.

---

## MARKER 7
### Develop and Deliver Lesson Plans for Teaching School-Wide Behavior Expectations and Rules

Develop lesson plans to teach school-wide behavior expectations and rules that include examples (appropriate behavior) and non-examples (inappropriate behaviors) in each setting. Deliver behavior lessons throughout the school year using a variety of teaching strategies. Teachers embed behavior teaching into their subject area curriculum on a daily basis.

## QUESTIONS TO CONSIDER

- Does our school have a behavior curriculum that includes lesson plans used to teach school-wide expectations and rules?
- Do the behavior lesson plans that our school developed include both examples of appropriate behavior (example) and examples of inappropriate behavior (non-example)?
- Do our lessons indicate the use of a variety of teaching strategies (at least three different strategies)?
- Do all our teachers embed behavior teaching into subject area curriculum on a daily basis?

- Are our staff and students involved in the development and delivery of behavior curriculum (lesson plans to teach behavior expectations and rules for specific settings)?
- Has our school developed and implemented strategies to share key features of our school-wide PBIS program with our families and community?

## Assessing Our Current State: Where Are We in Relation to Marker 7?

| Marker 7: Develop and Deliver Lesson Plans for Teaching School-Wide Behavior Expectations and Rules | 3 points | 2 points | 1 point | 0 points | Score |
|---|---|---|---|---|---|
| 29. A behavioral curriculum includes teaching behavior expectations and rules. | | Lesson plans **were** developed and used to teach behavior expectations and rules. | Lesson plans were developed and used to teach behavior expectations but **were not** developed for rules or vice versa. | Lesson plans **have not** been developed or used to teach behavior expectations or rules. | ___/2 |
| 30. Lessons include examples and non-examples. | | | Lesson plans **include** both examples of appropriate behavior and examples of inappropriate behavior. | Lesson plans give **no** specific examples or non-examples of appropriate behavior or there are no lesson plans. | ___/1 |
| 31. Lessons use a variety of teaching strategies. | | Lesson plans **are** taught using at least 3 different teaching strategies (i.e., modeling, role-playing, videotaping). | Lesson plans have been introduced using **fewer than** three teaching strategies. | Lesson plans **have not** been taught or do not exist. | ___/2 |
| 32. Lessons are embedded into subject area curriculum. | | **Nearly all** teachers embed behavior teaching into subject area curriculum on a daily basis. | **About 50 percent** of teachers embed behavior teaching into subject area | **Less than 50 percent** of all teachers embed behavior teaching into subject area | ___/2 |

*(Continued)*

(Continued)

| Marker 7: Develop and Deliver Lesson Plans for Teaching School-Wide Behavior Expectations and Rules | 3 points | 2 points | 1 point | 0 points | Score |
|---|---|---|---|---|---|
| | | | curriculum or embed behavior teaching fewer than three times per week. | curriculum or only occasionally remember to include behavior teaching in subject areas. | |
| 33. Faculty/staff members and students are involved in development and delivery of behavioral curriculum. | | | Faculty/staff members and students **are** involved in the development and delivery of lesson plans to teach behavior expectations and rules for specific settings. | Faculty/staff members and students **are not** involved in the development and delivery of lesson plans to teach behavior expectations and rules for specific settings. | ___/1 |
| 34. Strategies to share key features of school-wide PBIS plan with families/ community are developed and implemented. | | | The PBIS plan **includes** strategies to reinforce lessons with families and the community (i.e., after-school programs teach expectations, newsletters with tips for meeting expectations at home). | The PBIS plan **does not include** strategies to be used by families and the community. | ___/1 |

Source: Childs, Kincaid, & George (2011). Used with permission.

Our school's overall score for Marker 7 (Develop and Deliver Lesson Plans for Teaching School-Wide Behavior Expectations and Rules) is ___/9 points.

*(Note: The overall score is calculated by adding points given for each rubric statement.)*

---

**ACTIONS TO DEVELOP AND DELIVER LESSON PLANS FOR TEACHING SCHOOL-WIDE BEHAVIOR EXPECTATIONS AND RULES**

- Develop lesson plans to teach school-wide behavior expectations and rules that include examples (appropriate behavior) and non-examples (inappropriate behaviors) in each setting.

- The PBIS team, in collaboration with the administration, calendars school-wide teaching days at least twice a year to teach expectations and rules.
- The PBIS team shares the plan of how to teach expectations and rules with staff at the beginning of the school year.
- The PBIS team recruits students or teachers to help demonstrate the examples and non-examples in each setting.
- The PBIS team designs a plan for students who need additional small group instruction on expectations and rules.
- The PBIS team messages out to the parents and the community information about what the school is doing to teach the school-wide behavior expectations and rules.
- The teachers and the PBIS team deliver behavior lessons throughout the school year using a variety of teaching strategies.
- Teachers integrate behavior teaching into their subject area curriculum on a daily basis.
- The PBIS team schedules booster sessions (refresher behavior expectation and rule teaching opportunities) and reminders for staff to ensure the expectations and rules are integrated throughout the curricula as appropriate.
- Based on the behavior data of the school and input from community and staff, administration gives the PBIS team time to reflect on the feedback and data to strategize next steps to improve areas of identified need.

## OTHER ACTIONS TO CONSIDER

- Elicit student input on examples and non-examples for each setting.
- For middle schools and high schools, consider video announcements or targeting certain expectations and rules during homeroom or first period courses.
- Include leadership students in lesson plan development and delivery and/or video creation that would be relevant for their peers and focuses on teaching expectations and rules.

## CAUTION

If you find one or more of the following conditions or situations occurring at your school, view the condition or situation as a red flag that one or more areas of this marker—Develop and Deliver Lesson Plans for Teaching School-Wide Behavior Expectations and Rules—may need to be addressed.

## RED FLAGS

- The administrator informs teachers that they will be teaching an entire behavior curriculum in addition to new initiatives at the school.
- The PBIS team does not calendar school-wide teaching events.
- All staff (e.g., teachers, administration, classified, school psychologist) do not participate in the school-wide teaching events.
- Teacher, student, and other staff input is not collected throughout the year regarding the examples and non-examples that should be used to teach appropriate behavior, and examples and non-examples are not informed by data.

Based on our assessment of current state for this marker and the suggested list of actions and red flags, what should our next move be?

_____

_____

_____

_____

_____

_____

_____

_____

_____

_____

## FROM THE FIELD: MARKER 7—DEVELOP AND DELIVER LESSON PLANS FOR TEACHING SCHOOL-WIDE BEHAVIOR EXPECTATIONS AND RULES

**Challenge:** The PBIS team at the high school had been charged with messaging and teaching school-wide expectations to students daily. Daily announcements were a part of the school's structure and occasionally students would mention school-wide expectations in their announcements, but there was no daily consistency or easy guide for students to follow.

**Practical Solution:** The PBIS team met and developed a script in an easy format for leadership students to use when they made daily announcements. The script included school-wide expectations, a short pledge, and provided examples (appropriate demonstration of the expected behavior) and non-examples (inappropriate demonstration of the expected behavior). Each week, leadership students placed an emphasis on one school-wide expectation and described what it looked like in every setting. Leadership students read the script daily in morning announcements, and teachers *distributed caught being good tickets* to students demonstrating the school-wide expectation focus of the week. Every Friday, the leadership students selected five students who were recognized for demonstrating the school-wide expectations on morning announcements.

**Tool/Resource used:** Announcement Template for Teaching School-Wide Behavior Expectations and Rules (see Appendix B-7 in Appendix Resources B)

**What is it?** The announcement template is a graphic organizer to guide daily announcements focused on integrating daily teaching of school-wide behavior expectations and rules. The template includes school-wide behavior expectations, behavior examples and non-examples, and a short pledge. Each week there is a focus on a school-wide expectation and what it looks like in each setting.

### MARKER 8
### Develop and Deploy a School-Wide PBIS Implementation Plan

The PBIS team develops and deploys a school-wide PBIS implementation plan. The plan focuses on building staff capacity (knowledge and skill to execute). The plan includes the development and delivery of a curriculum to teach components of the discipline system to all staff; staff training on how to teach students expectations/rules and rewards; teaching students expectations/rules/rewards; booster sessions for students and staff; and an annual recognition schedule of rewards and incentives.

## QUESTIONS TO CONSIDER

- Has our school developed a curriculum to teach components of the discipline system to all staff, and is this curriculum used?
- Does our school have a plan for training all staff in our discipline system? Has our school developed and deployed a plan for training staff on how to teach students expectations and rules? Does our training include: plans to introduce the expectations and rules to all students, an explanation of how and when to use formal lesson plans, how to embed behavior teaching into daily curriculum, and how to execute our rewards and recognition program (type and frequency)?
- Has our school developed and deployed a plan for teaching students our school-wide expectations, rules, and rewards/recognition program?
- Does our school plan, schedule, and implement booster sessions for both students and staff for the purpose of reteaching? Do our booster sessions occur at least once in the year and additionally at times when the data suggest problems such as an increase in discipline referrals per day/per month or a high number of referrals in a specified area?
- Does our school review expectations and rules with students regularly (at least once per week)?
- Does our school have a plan for orienting incoming staff and students to our school-wide PBIS system? If yes, is our plan implemented throughout the year?
- Does our school have a plan for involving families and community in the development and ongoing implementation of PBIS? Is this plan executed?

### Assessing Our Current State:
### Where Are We in Relation to Marker 8

| Marker 8: Develop and Deploy a School-Wide PBIS Implementation Plan | 3 points | 2 points | 1 point | 0 points |
|---|---|---|---|---|
| 35. A curriculum to teach components of the discipline system to all faculty/staff members is | | The PBIS team scheduled time to present and train faculty/staff members on the discipline procedures and | The PBIS team scheduled time to present and train faculty/staff members on the discipline procedures and | Faculty/staff members either were not trained or were given the information **without** formal |

| Marker 8: Develop and Deploy a School-Wide PBIS Implementation Plan | 3 points | 2 points | 1 point | 0 points | Score |
|---|---|---|---|---|---|
| **developed and used.** | | data system, **including** checks for accuracy of information or comprehension. **Training included all components:** referral process (flowchart), definitions of problem behaviors, explanation of major vs. minor forms, and how the data will be used to guide the PBIS team in decision making. | data system, **but there were no** checks for accuracy of information or comprehension. **Training did not include all components:** referral process (flowchart), definitions of problem behaviors, explanation of major vs. minor forms, and how the data will be used to guide the PBIS team in decision making. | introduction and explanation. | |
| 36. **Plans for training faculty/staff members to teach students behavior expectations/rules and rewards are developed, scheduled, and delivered.** | | The PBIS team scheduled time to present and train faculty/staff members on lesson plans to teach students behavior expectations and rules **including** checks for accuracy of information or comprehension. **Training included all components:** plans to introduce the behavior expectations and rules to all students, explanation of how and when to use formal lesson plans, and how to embed behavior | The PBIS team scheduled time to present and train faculty/staff members on lesson plans to teach students behavior expectations and rules **but there were no** checks for accuracy of information or comprehension. **Training didn't include all components:** plans to introduce behavior expectations and rules to all students, explanation of how and when to use formal lesson plans, and how to embed behavior | Faculty/staff members either were not trained or were given the information **without** formal introduction and explanation. | ___/2 |

(Continued)

| Marker 8: Develop and Deploy a School-Wide PBIS Implementation Plan | 3 points | 2 points | 1 point | 0 points | Score |
|---|---|---|---|---|---|
| | | teaching into daily curriculum. | teaching into daily curriculum. | | |
| 37. A plan for teaching students behavior expectations/rules/rewards is developed, scheduled, and delivered. | Students are introduced/taught **all** of the following: school-wide behavior expectations, rules for specific settings, reward system guidelines. | Students are introduced/taught **two** of the following: school-wide behavior expectations, rules for specific settings, reward system guidelines. | Students are introduced/taught only **one** of the following: school-wide behavior expectations, rules for specific settings, reward system guidelines. | Students are not introduced/taught **any** of the following: school-wide behavior expectations, rules for specific settings, reward system guidelines. | ___/3 |
| 38. Booster sessions for students and faculty/staff members are planned, scheduled, and implemented. | | Booster sessions **are** planned and delivered to reteach faculty/staff/students at least once in the year and additionally at times when the data suggest problems by an increase in discipline referrals per day per month or a high number of referrals in a specified area. Behavior expectations and rules are reviewed with students regularly (at least 1 time per week). | Booster sessions **are not** utilized fully. For example: booster sessions are held for students but not faculty/staff members; booster sessions are held for faculty/staff members but not students; booster sessions are not held but behavior expectations and rules are reviewed at least weekly with students. | Booster sessions for students and faculty/staff members **are not** scheduled/planned. Behavior expectations and rules are reviewed with students once a month or less. | ___/2 |
| 39. The schedule for rewards/incentives for the year is planned. | | | There **is a** clear plan for the type and frequency of rewards/incentives to be delivered throughout the year. | There **is no** plan for the type and frequency of rewards/incentives to be delivered throughout the year. | ___/1 |

| ker 8: Develop Deploy a School-e PBIS lementation Plan | 3 points | 2 points | 1 point | 0 points | Score |
|---|---|---|---|---|---|
| **The plans for orienting incoming faculty/ staff members and students are developed and implemented.** | | The PBIS team **has** planned for and carries out the introduction of school-wide PBIS and training of new faculty/ staff members and students throughout the school year. | The PBIS team **has** planned for the introduction of school-wide PBIS and training of either new students or new faculty/staff members **but does not** include plans for training both, or the team has plans but has not implemented them. | The PBIS team **has not** planned for the introduction of school-wide PBIS and training of new faculty/ staff members or students. | ___/2 |
| **The plans for involving families/ community are developed and implemented.** | | | The PBIS team **has** planned the introduction to and ongoing engagement in school-wide PBIS for families/ community (i.e., newsletter, brochure, PTA, open-house, team member, etc.). | The PBIS team **has not** introduced school-wide PBIS to families/ community. | ___/1 |

Childs, Kincaid, & George (2011). Used with permission.

school's overall score for Marker 8 (Develop and Deploy a School-Wide PBIS Implementation Plan) is 3 points.

*The overall score is calculated by adding points given for each rubric statement.)*

---

### ACTIONS TO DEVELOP AND DEPLOY A SCHOOL-WIDE PBIS IMPLEMENTATION PLAN

- The PBIS team schedules time to present and train staff on the discipline procedures and data information system including checks for accuracy of information. Training includes all components: referral process (flowchart), definition of problem behaviors, explanation of major versus minor forms, and how the data will be used to guide the team in next steps (drive decision making). The PBIS team facilitates staff practice of procedures using authentic scenarios.

*(Continued)*

(Continued)

- The PBIS team schedules time to present and train staff on lesson plans to teach students expectations and rules including checks for accuracy of information or comprehension. Training includes all components: plans to introduce the expectations and rules to all students, explanation of how and when to use formal lesson plans, and how to embed behavior teaching into daily curriculum.
- Teach students the following: school expectations, rules for specific settings, and the reward system guidelines.
- The PBIS team calendars a portion of every staff meeting to discuss progress on the PBIS implementation plan.
- Plan and deliver booster sessions to reteach students and staff school-wide behavior expectations and rules, at least annually and additionally at times when the data indicates problems as evidenced by an increase in discipline referrals per day per month or a high number of referrals in a specified area. Regularly review the expectations and rules with students (at least weekly).
- Create a clear plan including the type and frequency of rewards/incentives to be given out throughout the year.
- The PBIS team plans for and carries out the introduction of school-wide PBIS and training of new staff and students throughout the school year.
- The PBIS team plans for the introduction and ongoing communication of school-wide PBIS to families and the community (i.e., newsletter, brochure, PTA, open house).

## OTHER ACTIONS TO CONSIDER

- Gather feedback from department heads on the behavior forms and behavior data collecting procedures aligned with the PBIS implementation plan.
- Assign an area in your school where the implementation plan is posted and resources and forms are available (some schools prefer to post or provide access to this information electronically while others prefer a PBIS wall in the office or staff lounge).
- Create a PBIS suggestion box in the office or staff lounge to provide staff ongoing input regarding PBIS implementation.

## CAUTION

If you find one or more of the following conditions or situations occurring at your school, view the condition or situation as a red flag that one or more areas of this marker—Develop and Deploy a School-Wide PBIS Implementation Plan—may need to be addressed.

## RED FLAGS

- The PBIS team has not trained staff on the implementation plan.
- The PBIS team does not calendar a portion of every staff meeting to discuss progress on the PBIS implementation plan.
- There are no plans to deliver booster sessions to reteach students and staff school-wide behavior expectations and rules, and no time is allocated to discuss data that indicate problems (i.e., data indicates an increase in discipline referrals per day per month or a high number of referrals in a specified area).
- Expectations and rules are not regularly reviewed with students.
- No clear plan exists for the type and frequency of rewards/incentives to be given out throughout the year.
- No plans exist to introduce and/or train new staff and students who enter the school throughout the year about school-wide PBIS.
- No plans exist to introduce school-wide PBIS to families and the community and provide for their ongoing involvement.
- Feedback from faculty or stakeholders is not used to drive next best decisions about PBIS implementation.
- The site administrator does not understand PBIS and directs staff to other administrators or individuals when questions arise about implementation.
- Staff are not updated throughout the year about the progress of the implementation plan.

Based on our assessment of current state for this marker and the suggested list of actions and red flags, what should our next move be?

_____

_____

_____

_____

*(Continued)*

(Continued)

_____

_____

_____

_____

_____

_____

⁂

## FROM THE FIELD: MARKER 8— DEVELOP AND DEPLOY A SCHOOL-WIDE PBIS IMPLEMENTATION PLAN

**Challenge:** The PBIS team was overwhelmed by what they needed to do throughout the year. They asked for a year-at-a-glance template to help get them organized, simplify planning, and serve as a resource that they could share with staff.

**Practical Solution:** The PBIS district coordinator created a Year at a Glance—Monthly Action Plan Template to help organize and guide the PBIS team in deploying their monthly actions. The PBIS team members used this template to guide them in the actions they needed to take each month as well as used this tool to help them communicate with staff about the actions being deployed.

**Tool/Resource used:** Year at a Glance—Monthly Action Plan Template (see Appendix B-8 in Appendix Resources B)

**What is it?** The Year at a Glance—Monthly Action Plan Template is an organizational tool that guides the PBIS team in prioritizing monthly actions throughout a school year.

---

**MARKER 9**
**Establish Classroom Systems—Routines/Procedures**

Teachers establish a system of what is expected in their classrooms relative to the school-wide behavior expectations. Behaviors are taught in each classroom—(a) classroom rules for each school-wide expectation are clearly defined and posted and (b) classroom procedures and routines for activities where problems often occur (i.e., using the restrooms or entering the classroom) are explicitly identified. Procedures exist for tracking classroom behavior problems. As part of the classroom system, teachers use immediate and specific praise, acknowledge students demonstrating adherence to classroom rules and routines, and use a range of consequences/interventions for problem behavior that are documented and consistently delivered. *(Note: This acknowledgment of appropriate behaviors occurs more frequently than the acknowledgment of inappropriate behaviors.)*

## QUESTIONS TO CONSIDER

- Have all teachers in our school established a classroom system where (a) classroom rules are clearly defined and posted for each school-wide behavior expectation and (b) classroom procedures and routines are explicitly identified for activities where problems often occur such as using the restrooms or entering the classroom?
- What evidence exists at our school that the behavior routines expected in each classroom have been taught and reviewed and are reinforced throughout the year?
- Do all our teachers use immediate and specific praise? What evidence exists?
- Do all our teachers acknowledge students demonstrating adherence to classroom rules and routines, and does this acknowledgment occur more frequently than acknowledgment of inappropriate behaviors?
- Do procedures exist in each of our classrooms to track classroom behavior problems?
- Do all our teachers use a range of classroom consequences/ interventions for problem behavior, and are these consequences/ interventions documented and consistently applied?

## Assessing Our Current State:
## Where Are We in Relation to Marker 9?

| Marker 9: Establish Classroom Systems—Routines/Procedures | 3 points | 2 points | 1 point | 0 points | Score |
|---|---|---|---|---|---|
| 42. Classroom rules are defined for each of the school-wide behavior expectations and are posted in classrooms. | | Evident in most classrooms (**more than 75 percent** of classrooms). | Evident in many classrooms (**at least 50 to 75 percent** of classrooms). | Evident in only a few classrooms (**fewer than 50 percent** of classrooms). | ___/2 |
| 43. Classroom routines and procedures are explicitly identified for activities where problems often occur (e.g. entering class, asking questions, sharpening pencil, using restroom, dismissal). | | Evident in most classrooms (**more than 75 percent** of classrooms). | Evident in many classrooms (**at least 50 to 75 percent** of classrooms). | Evident in only a few classrooms (**fewer than 50 percent** of classrooms). | ___/2 |
| 44. Expected behavior routines in classrooms are taught. | | Evident in most classrooms (**more than 75 percent** of classrooms). | Evident in many classrooms (**at least 50 to 75 percent** of classrooms). | Evident in only a few classrooms (**fewer than 50 percent** of classrooms). | ___/2 |
| 45. Classroom teachers use immediate and specific praise. | | Evident in most classrooms (**more than 75 percent** of classrooms). | Evident in many classrooms (**at least 50 to 75 percent** of classrooms). | Evident in only a few classrooms (**fewer than 50 percent** of classrooms). | ___/2 |
| 46. Acknowledgement of students demonstrating adherence to classroom rules and routines occurs more frequently than acknowledgement of inappropriate behaviors. | | Evident in most classrooms (**more than 75 percent** of classrooms). | Evident in many classrooms (**at least 50 to 75 percent** of classrooms). | Evident in only a few classrooms (**fewer than 50 percent** of classrooms). | ___/2 |
| 47. Procedures exist for tracking classroom behavior problems. | | Evident in most classrooms **more than 75 percent** of classrooms). | Evident in many classrooms (**at least 50 to 75 percent** of classrooms). | Evident in only a few classrooms (**fewer than 50 percent** of classrooms). | ___/2 |

| Marker 9: Establish Classroom Systems—Routines/Procedures | 3 points | 2 points | 1 point | 0 points | Score |
|---|---|---|---|---|---|
| 48. Classrooms have a range of consequences/ interventions for problem behavior that are documented and consistently delivered. | | Evident in most classrooms (**more than 75 percent** of classrooms). | Evident in many classrooms (**at least 50 to 75 percent** of classrooms). | Evident in only a few classrooms (**fewer than 50 percent** of classrooms). | ___/2 |

*Source:* Childs, Kincaid, & George (2011). Used with permission.

Our school's overall score for Marker 9 (Establish Classroom Systems—Routines/Procedures) is __/14 points.

*(Note: The overall score is calculated by adding points given for each rubric statement.)*

---

**ACTIONS TO ESTABLISH CLASSROOM SYSTEMS—ROUTINES/PROCEDURES**

- The PBIS team gathers feedback from staff and develops draft classroom routines to help guide teachers in classroom system development.
- Classroom teachers define and post classroom rules aligned with school-wide behavior expectations. The PBIS team provides samples for teachers to reference.
- The PBIS team researches and provides resources for teachers to help them teach routines and procedures to students using a variety of strategies.
- Classroom teachers define and teach classroom routines and procedures.
- The PBIS team is allocated time to research and present resources to teachers at staff trainings on classroom consequences and interventions as well as various approaches for acknowledging students.
- Classroom teachers are equipped with and use a range of interventions/ consequences for classroom behaviors.
- Classroom teachers praise and acknowledge students for appropriate behavior more frequently than acknowledging inappropriate behavior.
- Classroom teachers design and deploy a behavior tracking system in the classroom.
- The PBIS team gathers data regarding the visibility in all classrooms of school-wide behavior expectations and aligned classroom rules.
- The PBIS team reminds teachers to review their classroom system procedures quarterly and gather input and feedback from students on ways to meaningfully acknowledge progress and success.

## OTHER ACTIONS TO CONSIDER

- Task a group of teachers to work collaboratively to create a good frame for other teachers to use to establish their classroom systems.
- Include classroom system information on syllabi, school agenda, or in the weekly packet/communication to parents.
- Gather student input on what type of acknowledgment is meaningful to them.
- Observe a teacher with a strong classroom system, collect specific evidence/data about what makes the system strong, and discuss the evidence in school teams.
- Elicit student input to help identify procedures and routines.
- As part of a substitute teacher's plan, require teachers to include classroom rules, procedures, and how to acknowledge students behaving appropriately.

## CAUTION

If you find one or more of the following conditions or situations occurring at your school, view the condition or situation as a red flag that one or more areas of this marker—Establish Classroom Systems—Routines/Procedures—may need to be addressed.

### RED FLAGS

- Classroom teachers are not provided time or resources to develop their classroom rules, routines, and procedures.
- Classroom teachers do not have rules posted in their classrooms.
- Classroom teachers do not teach rules, routines, and procedures in their classrooms.
- Classroom teachers do not use an array of consequences and interventions in their classrooms.
- Classroom teachers acknowledge negative behavior more than positive behavior.
- The PBIS team is not provided time to research and provide resources for classroom teachers on classroom management and support.
- Classroom teachers do not acknowledge students for positive behavior.
- Classroom teachers do not have a system for tracking behavior in their classroom.
- Teachers are given specific rules and routines that must be used in their classrooms.
- Teachers who need help setting up their classroom systems are not supported.
- Teachers do not refer to posted expectations and rules.

❧❧❧

Based on our assessment of current state for this marker and the suggested list of actions and red flags, what should our next move be?

_____

_____

_____

_____

_____

_____

_____

_____

_____

❧❧❧

## FROM THE FIELD: MARKER 9—ESTABLISH CLASSROOM SYSTEMS—ROUTINES/PROCEDURES

**Challenge:** A school PBIS team was assigned the task of developing a set of classroom rules aligned with the school-wide expectations that would be used by all classroom teachers. The school staff voiced that they wanted a say in what the rules were in their classrooms.

**Practical Solution:** The PBIS team asked all teachers to fill out a blank classroom rules grid indicating the rules that they would like to see used for each of the school-wide behavior expectations. The PBIS team asked the staff to indicate their top five classroom rules positively stated. The PBIS team used an affinity process of grouping like ideas to create a set of classroom rules for each of the school-wide behavior expectations. The PBIS team created a grid that included the school-wide expectations, set of classroom rules, and examples and non-examples of the expected behavior. The teachers then used these grids to teach the expectations and rules to their students. These grids were also enlarged and posted in classrooms for daily reference. In addition, the classroom rules became a part of every classroom's syllabus.

**Tool/Resource used:** Classroom Rules Grid and Affinity Process (see Appendix B-9 in Appendix Resources B)

**What is it?** Blank template used to gather individual input regarding desired classroom rules in alignment with school-wide behavior expectation. An affinity process was used to gather data quickly, group like ideas, and ensure that all voices were heard.

---

## MARKER 10
## Establish and Execute an Evaluation Plan

The PBIS team designs and executes a plan to evaluate PBIS implementation and system effectiveness.

### QUESTIONS TO CONSIDER

- Does our school survey students and staff specifically about our school-wide PBIS plan and level of implementation? If yes, is this survey data turned into information and used for continuous system improvement?
- Does our school have evidence that all students and staff can identify our school-wide expectations and rules for specific settings? If yes, what type of evidence has our school collected? What instruments are used to collect this evidence?
- Does all staff use our referral process (including which behaviors are office managed versus which are teacher managed) and forms appropriately?
- Does all staff know our school procedures for responding to inappropriate behavior, use forms as intended, and fill forms out accurately? What evidence indicates progress and success in this area?
- Has our school identified guidelines for our reward system? Does all staff understand the guidelines for our reward/recognition system and use the reward system appropriately? What evidence indicates progress and success in this area?
- Has our school developed a plan for the collection and analysis of data to evaluate PBIS outcomes? If yes, is the plan deployed and are data collected as scheduled and used to evaluate the PBIS plan?
- Are outcomes regarding such areas as behavior problems, attendance, and morale documented and used to evaluate our PBIS plan?

## Assessing Our Current State:
## Where Are We in Relation to Marker 10?

| Marker 10: Establish and Execute an Evaluation Plan | 3 points | 2 points | 1 point | 0 points | Score |
|---|---|---|---|---|---|
| 49. **Students and faculty/staff members are surveyed about PBIS.** | | Students and faculty/staff members **are** surveyed at least annually (i.e. items on climate survey or specially developed PBIS plan survey), and information **is used** to address the PBIS plan. | Students and faculty/staff members **are** surveyed at least annually (i.e. items on climate survey or specially developed PBIS plan survey), but information **is not used** to address the PBIS plan. | Students and faculty/staff members **are not** surveyed. | ___/2 |
| 50. **Students and faculty/staff members can identify behavior expectations and rules.** | | **Almost all** students and faculty/staff members can identify the school-wide behavior expectations and rules for specific settings (can be identified through surveys, random interviews, etc.), and (**at least 90 percent** know/ use). | **Many** students and faculty/staff members can identify the school-wide behavior expectations and rules for specific settings (**at least 50 percent** know/ use). | **Few** students and faculty/staff members can identify the school-wide behavior expectations and rules for specific settings or no evaluation is conducted in this area (**less than 50 percent** know/ use). | ___/2 |
| 51. **Faculty/staff members use referral process (including which behaviors are office managed vs. which are teacher managed) and use forms appropriately.** | **Almost all** faculty/ staff members know the procedures for responding to inappropriate behavior, use forms as intended, and fill them out correctly (can be identified by reviewing completed forms, staff surveys, etc.), and (**at least 90 percent** know/use). | **Many** of the faculty/staff members know the procedures for responding to inappropriate behavior, use forms as intended, and fill them out correctly (**at least 75 percent** know/ use). | **Some** of the faculty/staff members know the procedures for responding to inappropriate behavior, use forms as intended, and fill them out correctly (at **least 50 percent** know/ use). | **Few** faculty/staff members know the procedures for responding to inappropriate behavior, use forms as intended, and fill them out correctly or no evaluation is conducted in this area (**less than 50 percent** know/ use). | ___/3 |

*(Continued)*

(Continued)

| Marker 10: Establish and Execute an Evaluation Plan | 3 points | 2 points | 1 point | 0 points | Score |
|---|---|---|---|---|---|
| 52. **Faculty/staff members use reward system appropriately.** | **Almost all** faculty/staff members understand identified guidelines for the reward system and are using the reward system appropriately (can be identified by reviewing reward token distribution, surveys, etc.), and **at least 90 percent** understand/use. | **Many** of the faculty/staff members understand identified guidelines for the reward system and are using the reward system appropriately (**at least 75 percent** understand/use). | **Some** of the faculty/staff members understand identified guidelines for the reward system and are using the reward system appropriately (**at least 50 percent** understand/use). | **Few** faculty/staff members understand and use identified guidelines for the reward system or evaluation is not conducted at least annually in this area or staff knowledge and use of the reward system is not assessed (**less than 50 percent** understand/use). | __/3 |
| 53. **Outcomes (behavior problems, attendance, and morale) are documented and used to evaluate PBIS plan.** | There is a plan for collecting data to evaluate PBIS outcomes, **most** data are collected as scheduled, and data are used to evaluate PBIS plan. | There is a plan for collecting data to evaluate PBIS outcomes, **some** of the scheduled data have been collected, and data are used to evaluate PBIS plan. | There is a plan for collecting data to evaluate PBIS outcomes; however **nothing** has been collected to date. | There is **no** plan for collecting data to evaluate PBIS outcomes. | __/3 |

Source: Childs, Kincaid, & George (2011). Used with permission.

Our school's overall score for Marker 10 (Establish and Execute an Evaluation Plan) is __/13 points.

(*Note: The overall score is calculated by adding points given for each rubric statement.*)

---

**ACTIONS TO ESTABLISH AND EXECUTE AN EVALUATION PLAN**

- The PBIS team develops a plan for the collection and analysis of data to evaluate PBIS outcomes. Deploy the plan, collect the data as scheduled, and use the data to evaluate the PBIS plan.
- The PBIS team educates the staff on the evaluation plan—purpose of evaluation and who will be involved, data collection procedures, instruments used such as survey, and so forth.

- Survey students and staff, at least annually, about the school-wide PBIS plan and level of implementation. Turn survey data into information, and use it for continuous system improvement.
- Collect data indicating the number/percentage of students and staff who can articulate the established school-wide expectations. Develop instruments to collect, analyze, and share this data.
- Appropriately use the referral process and forms. Monitor the process for appropriate use (including which behaviors are office managed vs. which are teacher managed).
- Educate all staff on school procedures for responding to inappropriate behavior, appropriate use of forms, and accurate completion of forms. Collect data indicating the number/percentage of staff who know the procedures for responding to inappropriate behavior, use forms as intended, and complete forms accurately. Develop indicators that evidence progress and success in this area.
- Identify guidelines for a school reward/recognition system. Educate all staff on the guidelines of the reward/recognition system, and use the system appropriately. Collect data indicating the number/percentage of staff who can articulate the guidelines for the reward/recognition system and use the system appropriately. Develop indicators that evidence progress and success in this area.

## OTHER ACTIONS TO CONSIDER

- Provide time during staff meetings or department meetings for PBIS survey completion and feedback.

## CAUTION

If you find one or more of the following conditions or situations occurring at your school, view the condition or situation as a red flag that one or more areas of this marker—Establish and Execute an Evaluation Plan—may need to be addressed.

### RED FLAGS

- Students and staff are not surveyed on an annual basis on PBIS implementation.
- Survey data are not used to help make decisions about PBIS implementation.

*(Continued)*

(Continued)

- No data are collected indicating the number/percentage of students and staff who can articulate the established school-wide expectations.
- Instruments are not developed to help collect, analyze, and share evaluation data.
- The office discipline referral process is inappropriately used and forms are inaccurately completed.
- No one is designated to monitor the collection process (including which behaviors are office managed vs. which are teacher managed).
- Staff are not educated on school procedures for responding to inappropriate behavior, appropriate use of forms, and accurate completion of forms.
- No guidelines or written documentation exist for a school-wide behavior reward/recognition system.
- Staff are not educated on the behavior reward/recognition system.
- Staff uses the reward/recognition system inappropriately or applies it inconsistently.
- The PBIS team is not provided time to gather data and train staff on implementation.
- No plan is developed and shared with staff on the collection and analysis of data to evaluate PBIS outcomes.

Based on our assessment of current state for this marker and the suggested list of actions and red flags, what should our next move be?

_____

_____

_____

_____

_____

_____

_____

_____

_____

_____

_____

## FROM THE FIELD: MARKER 10— ESTABLISH AND EXECUTE AN EVALUATION PLAN

**Challenge:** A PBIS team was assigned the task of developing a PBIS evaluation plan. They were unclear about what data to gather because they had not established intended outcomes as a team. The PBIS team was unsure of how to approach this task.

**Practical Solution:** The PBIS team members worked with their district PBIS coordinator to design a simple data collection schedule to help them evaluate implementation. This tool helped the PBIS team identify and organize what data needed to be collected and by when. This data collection schedule also ensured that both baseline and follow up assessment data were collected.

**Tool/Resource used:** Positive Behavior Interventions and Supports (PBIS) Data Collection Schedule (see Appendix B-10 in Appendix Resources B)

**What is it?** A schedule detailing what data are to be collected, when data are to be collected, what instrument will be used to collect the data, and who is involved in data collection

## OVERVIEW OF CATEGORY A RESULTS: TIER 1 PBIS MARKERS

| Category A: Tier 1 PBIS Markers | What is your score? |
|---|---|
| Category A: Scores for Tier 1 PBIS Markers | |
| Marker 1: Establish and Operate an Effective PBIS Team | ____/6 |
| Marker 2: Establish and Maintain Faculty/Staff Commitment | ____/6 |
| Marker 3: Establish and Deploy Effective Procedures for Dealing with Discipline | ____/11 |
| Marker 4: Establish a Data Entry Procedure & Design an Analysis Plan | ____/8 |
| Marker 5: Establish a Set of School-Wide Behavior Expectations and Rules | ____/11 |
| Marker 6: Establish a Behavior Reward/ Recognition Program | ____/16 |
| Marker 7: Develop and Deliver Lesson Plans for Teaching School-Wide Behavior Expectations and Rules | ____/9 |
| Marker 8: Develop and Deploy a School-Wide PBIS Implementation Plan | ____/13 |
| Marker 9: Establish Classroom Systems - Routines/Procedures | ____/14 |
| Marker 10: Establish and Execute an Evaluation Plan | ____/13 |
| | Total Score:<br><br>____/107<br><br>**Note:** *The goal is 80 percent or higher. Divide your total points by the points possible to get the percentage.* |

# Getting Started With Category B— Tier 1 School-Wide Characteristics

**T**his chapter identifies and describes the Tier 1 school-wide characteristics of a Bronze Positive Behavior Interventions and Supports (PBIS) Champion Model System, guides you through an assessment of your current state, presents challenges from the field with practical solutions, and prompts reflection based on assessment data about next-step actions to move your system from current state to desired future—Bronze PBIS Champion Model System.

So what are the four Tier 1 school-wide characteristics? The four primary school-wide characteristics are as follows:

1. Existence of school-wide behavior expectations

2. Visibility of school-wide behavior expectations and rules in multiple settings

3. Student knowledge of school-wide behavior expectations

4. Staff knowledge of school-wide behavior expectations and other Tier 1 PBIS markers

In order to build a strong Tier 1 PBIS foundation, the four school-wide characteristics must be solidly evident. These characteristics can best be captured and assessed through an adapted version of Florida's Positive Behavior Support (PBS) Project On-site PBIS:RtIB Walkthrough form (Florida PBS project). This process and tool was originally designed to gather evidence of PBIS implementation through observation and conversation with students and staff in schools. It provides a school view or state of the school relative to a school-wide proactive discipline and systems approach to defining, teaching, and supporting appropriate student behaviors that create positive school environments. This walkthrough process, which takes approximately twenty-five minutes, should at minimum be conducted at the beginning of the year to collect PBIS baseline data and then again at the end of the year to measure progress and success.

**Who should conduct the On-Site PBIS Tier 1 Walkthrough?** To obtain accurate baseline information, first look to an external assessor such as a person from the district office trained in PBIS. If your district does not have an identified person who supports the PBIS work in schools, the site administrator in collaboration with the PBIS coach should conduct the walkthrough assessment.

**How will this data be used?** You will use the results of this walkthrough to perform a gap analysis and get a better understanding of where your system is in relation to the four primary school-wide characteristics. You will calculate points for each school-wide characteristic. Total possible points is 37, and the scoring scale is as follows: 30–37 points = the system is on target with the school-wide characteristics, 15–29 points = the system is making progress with the school-wide characteristics, and 0–14 points = the system is in need of improvement with the school-wide characteristics.

| On Target | 30–37 points |
|---|---|
| Making Progress | 15–29 points |
| Need Improvement | 0–14 points |

The indicator evidencing a strong Tier 1 foundation is an overall walkthrough score in the 30–37 on target point range. This walkthrough data should be part of the school's data or information management system and used as another important information stream to inform next steps. Therefore, it is important that objective responses are provided. You can locate the entire On-Site PBIS Tier 1 Walkthrough form (Adapted Version and Scoring Scale) in Appendix Resources A section A-4. We use the results from the on-site walkthrough as one measure to evidence attainment of a Tier 1 Bronze PBIS Champion Model System.

A first step toward developing a Tier 1 Bronze PBIS Champion Model System is to assess the current state of your own system and then identify next-step, high-leverage actions based on data analysis, taking into consideration not only data from your on-site walkthrough but the results of your ten critical Maker assessments (Category A—Chapter 3). The next section of this chapter guides you through a quick assessment (Florida's Positive Behavior Support Project, n.d.) of each school-wide characteristic, provides you with the opportunity to reflect on next steps, and presents challenges and practical solutions from the field.

---

### School-Wide Characteristic 1:
### Existence of School-Wide Behavior Expectations

The school has established three to five positively stated school-wide behavior expectations that embrace the core values of the system.

## ASSESSING OUR CURRENT STATE: WHERE ARE WE IN RELATION TO THIS SCHOOL-WIDE CHARACTERISTIC?

*Does our school have three to five positively stated school-wide behavior expectations? If yes, what are they?* Write the school-wide behavior expectations in the space below.

### School-Wide Behavior Expectations

1.

2.

3.

4.

5.

━━━━━━━━━━━━━━━━━━━━━━━━━━ ❧❧ ━━━━━━━━━━━━━━━━━━━━━━━━━━

**What is our score?** Calculate 1 point if three to five positively stated school-wide behavior expectations exist and 0 points if they do not exist. ＿＿＿/1

━━━━━━━━━━━━━━━━━━━━━━━━━━ ❧❧ ━━━━━━━━━━━━━━━━━━━━━━━━━━

**What next?** Refer to Marker 5—Establish a Set of School-Wide Behavior Expectations and Rules (Chapter 3).

━━━━━━━━━━━━━━━━━━━━━━━━━━ ❧❧ ━━━━━━━━━━━━━━━━━━━━━━━━━━

What actions should we take to move our school closer to target on this school-wide characteristic?

_____

_____

_____

_____

_____

_____

_____

_____

_____

_____

_____

━━━━━━━━━━━━━━━━━━━━━━━━━━ ❧❧ ━━━━━━━━━━━━━━━━━━━━━━━━━━

## FROM THE FIELD: SCHOOL-WIDE CHARACTERISTIC 1

**Challenge:** A middle school was in the very beginning stages of PBIS implementation, and the PBIS team expressed concern that they did not have any idea about what a school-wide behavior expectation might look like and sound like.

**Practical solution:** The district office PBIS coordinator developed a list of sample school-wide behavior expectations to help guide the PBIS team in development of their school-wide behavior expectations. The district coordinator included the following tips: Make the expectations short and easy to remember. Try to connect the expectations to something that students and staff will remember such as Strive for FIve (Be Respectful, Be Safe, Work Peacefully, Strive for Excellence, and Follow Directions). Identify a signal or nonverbal representation such as for Five—open hand of five fingers, each finger representing a school-wide behavior expectation.

**Tool/Resource used:** List of Sample School-Wide Behavior Expectations (Appendix B-11, Appendix Resources B)

---

### School-Wide Characteristic 2: Visibility of School-Wide Behavior Expectations and Rules in Multiple Settings

Visibility of school-wide behavior expectations and rules in multiple settings means that positively stated school-wide behavior expectations with a set of directly aligned positively stated rules are enlarged (posters, banners, signs, etc.) and posted/placed in all classrooms and in at least six different settings throughout the school. The posters, banners, and/or signs need to be big enough for the students and staff to notice on a daily basis in classrooms and other settings (hallways, gym/playground, main office(s), cafeteria, and library) as well as in at least one other area that is an important setting for your school. *(Note: The school-wide behavior expectations are the umbrella and the rules are what the expectations look like in each setting stated in a positive manner. For example, the school-wide expectation is respect, and the classroom rules under respect are to listen to the teacher, raise your hand before you speak, etc.)*

---

## ASSESSING OUR CURRENT STATE: WHERE ARE WE IN RELATION TO SCHOOL-WIDE CHARACTERISTIC 2?

### Visibility (includes 2 parts)

#### *Visibility in Multiple Settings Outside the Classroom (Part 1)*

*Has our school enlarged our school-wide behavior expectations, and are these expectations/rules posted in at least six settings throughout our school?* Walk around the school campus, and assess the visibility of your school-wide behavior expectations in at least six settings. Indicate where your school-wide behavior expectations and rules are visibly located.

Indicate ☑ where **expectations/rules** are visible:

| | | |
|---|---|---|
| Library ☐ | Hallways ☐ | Main Office(s) ☐ |
| Cafeteria ☐ | Gym/Playground ☐ | Other ☐ |

**What is our score?** Calculate 1 point for each different kind of location where the school-wide behavior expectations/rules are visibly posted and would be noticed on a daily basis. Up to 6 points can be earned in this area. _____/6

### Visibility in Classrooms (Part 2)

Walk through at least five classrooms around the school campus (a variety of classrooms/grades/subjects), and assess the visibility of rules aligned to the school-wide behavior expectations.

Indicate how many of the five classrooms had visibly posted rules aligned to the school-wide behavior expectations. Circle the number of classrooms.

1 2 3 4 5 classrooms

**What is our score?** Calculate 1 point for each classroom with visibly posted rules aligned to the school-wide behavior expectations. Up to 5 points can be earned in this area. _____/5

Total Part 1 and Part 2 Score: _____/11

**What next?** Refer to the following three markers in Chapter 3:

- Marker 5: Establish a Set of Behavior Expectations and Rules
- Marker 9: Establish Classroom Systems—Routines/Procedures
- Marker 10: Establish and Execute an Evaluation Plan

---

What actions should we take to move our school closer to target on this school-wide characteristic?

_____

_____

_____

_____

_____

_____

_____

---

## FROM THE FIELD: SCHOOL-WIDE CHARACTERISTIC 2

**Challenge:** A new school implementing PBIS was unclear on how to make the school-wide expectations visible in each setting.

**Practical solution:** A district-designated person who supports PBIS work in schools gathered pictures/visuals (posters, banners, signs, etc.) that Champion Model Schools had posted around their campuses in multiple settings. The PBIS team used these as samples for banner and sign companies that they hired to assist them in their visual designs.

**Tool/Resource used:** Pictures/Visuals Posted at Champion Model Schools (Appendix B-12, Appendix Resources B)

### School-Wide Characteristic 3: Student Knowledge of School-Wide Behavior Expectations

Student knowledge means every student can articulate the school-wide behavior expectations.

## ASSESSING OUR CURRENT STATE: WHERE ARE WE IN RELATION TO THIS SCHOOL-WIDE CHARACTERISTIC?

*Do all the students on our campus know our school-wide behavior expectations, and can they articulate them when asked?* Ask five randomly selected students (from a variety of classes/grades/subjects) to recite the school-wide behavior expectations.

❧❧

**Students:** Indicate how many students (of five) are able to tell you **all** the expectations.
1  2  3  4  5  student(s)

❧❧

**What is our score?** Calculate 1 point for each student who can articulate all the school-wide behavior expectations. Up to 5 points can be earned in this area. *(Note: If a student can articulate only three of five expectations, no point is given.)* _____/5

❧❧

**What next?** Refer to the following markers in Chapter 3:

- Marker 5: Establish a Set of School-Wide Behavior Expectations and Rules
- Marker 6: Establish a Behavior Reward/Recognition Program
- Marker 7: Develop and Deliver Lesson Plans for Teaching School-Wide Behavior Expectations and Rules
- Marker 8: Develop and Deploy a School-Wide PBIS Implementation Plan
- Marker 9: Establish Classroom Systems—Routines/Procedures
- Marker 10: Establish and Execute an Evaluation Plan

❧❧

What actions should we take to move our school closer to target on this school-wide characteristic?

_____

_____

_____

_____

❧❧

## FROM THE FIELD: SCHOOL-WIDE CHARACTERISTIC 3

**Challenge:** A PBIS team of a large comprehensive high school was overwhelmed by the thought and expectation that every student on campus must learn and be able to articulate all school-wide behavior expectations. They were unsure of what approach or approaches would be the most effective to use to educate all students.

**Practical solution:** The PBIS team gathered input from the students (student voice) on the best methods to use to effectively teach all students the school-wide expectations. Based on student input, two school-wide teaching days with resources were developed with student assistance.

**Tool/Resource used:** Positive Behavior Interventions and Supports (PBIS) Teaching Day Memo—Guide for School-Wide Teaching Days (Appendix B-13, Appendix Resources B)

---

### School-Wide Characteristic 4: Staff Knowledge of School-Wide Behavior Expectations and Other Tier 1 PBIS Markers

Staff knowledge of school-wide behavior expectations means every staff member can articulate the school-wide behavior expectations. Staff knowledge of other Tier 1 PBIS markers means all staff members can articulate the names of the school's PBIS team members (school-wide team to address behavior/discipline across campus), affirm they have taught the school-wide behavior expectations in a variety of settings, and confirm they have seen the school's discipline data throughout the school year.

## ASSESSING OUR CURRENT STATE: WHERE ARE WE IN RELATION TO THIS SCHOOL-WIDE CHARACTERISTIC?

- Can every staff member at our school name all members of our PBIS team (school-wide team that addresses behavior/discipline across campus)?
- Can every staff member at our school articulate all school-wide behavior expectations?
- Can every staff member at our school evidence that he/she has taught our school-wide behavior expectations in a variety of settings?
- Has every staff member been provided our school's discipline data throughout the school year?

Ask five randomly selected staff members serving in various roles at the school such as teacher, certificated support (i.e., school psychologist, nurse), custodian, office personnel, food service, and administration the following four questions regarding PBIS school-wide characteristics:

**Staff** (Ask five staff members the following questions.)

Do you have a PBIS team to address behavior/discipline across campus? Please name the members of the team.

Indicate how many staff know about the team and can articulate the team members' names.

1 2 3 4 5

Do you know all the school-wide behavior expectations? If yes, please state them.

Indicate how many staff are able to tell you **all** the expectations.

1 2 3 4 5

Have you taught the school-wide behavior expectations in a variety of settings? If yes, please give one example of how an expectation was taught and in what setting.

Indicate how many staff report teaching **all** school-wide behavior expectations in a variety of settings.

1 2 3 4 5

Have you seen the school's discipline data this year?

Indicate how many staff report seeing the data.

1 2 3 4 5

**What is our score?** Calculate 1 point for each accurate response. A maximum of 4 points per staff member can be earned. Up to 20 points can be earned in this area (4 points/per staff member x 5 staff members = 20 points). *(Note: If a staff member can articulate only 3 of 5 expectations, no point is given.)* _____/20

**What next?** Refer to all markers in Chapter 3 specific to the assessed area of need:

- Marker 1: Establish and Operate an Effective PBIS Team
- Marker 2: Establish and Maintain Faculty/Staff Commitment

- Marker 3: Establish and Deploy Effective Procedures for Dealing with Discipline
- Marker 4: Establish a Data Entry Procedure and Design an Analysis Plan
- Marker 5: Establish a Set of School-Wide Behavior Expectations and Rules
- Marker 6: Establish a Behavior Reward/Recognition Program
- Marker 7: Develop and Deliver Lesson Plans for Teaching School-Wide Behavior Expectations and Rules
- Marker 8: Develop and Deploy a School-Wide PBIS Implementation Plan
- Marker 9: Establish Classroom Systems—Routines/Procedures
- Marker 10: Establish and Execute an Evaluation Plan

What actions should we take to move our school closer to target on this school-wide characteristic?

_____

_____

_____

_____

_____

_____

_____

_____

_____

_____

## FROM THE FIELD: SCHOOL-WIDE CHARACTERISTIC 4

**Challenge:** A PBIS team wanted an ongoing communication method to keep staff informed on PBIS information related to the school (e.g., behavior data, members of the team, next-step plans, research, resources).

**Practical solution:** The PBIS team designated a wall in the staff lounge as the PBIS communication board for the purpose of updating the staff on a regular basis about what was happening in regard to PBIS implementation at their school as well as to hold staff accountable for reviewing behavior data.

**Tool/Resource used:** Staff Positive Behavior Interventions and Supports (PBIS) Communication Wall—Sample Picture (Appendix B-14, found in Appendix Resources B)

## OVERVIEW OF CATEGORY B RESULTS: TIER 1 SCHOOL-WIDE CHARACTERISTICS

| Category B: Tier 1 School-Wide Characteristics | What is your score? |
|---|---|
| Category B: Tier 1 School-Wide Characteristics Score | |
| 1. Existence of School-Wide Behavior Expectations | _____/1 |
| 2. Visibility of School-Wide Behavior Expectations and Rules in Multiple Settings | _____/11 |
| 3. Student Knowledge of School-Wide Behavior Expectations | _____/5 |
| 4. Staff Knowledge of School-Wide Behavior Expectations and Other Tier 1 PBIS Markers | _____/20 |
| **On Target** 30–37 points<br>**Making Progress** 15–29 points<br>**Need Improvement** 0–14 points | Total Score:<br>_____/37 |

# Getting Started With Category C— Tier 1 School-Wide Academic/ Behavioral Goals and the Work of the PBIS Team

**T**o be a Champion Model PBIS (Positive Behavior Interventions and Supports) System, a school must demonstrate school-wide positive change in academic and behavioral results aligned with PBIS initiatives and goals. Specifically, a school must establish and achieve academic and behavioral goals required of each tier:

- Tier 1: The Bronze level requires that at least one school-wide academic and behavioral SMART goal be established and achieved.
- Tier 2: The Silver level requires that the Tier 1 goals be met plus at least one small-group academic and behavioral SMART goal be established and achieved for students not responding to Tier 1.

- Tier 3: The Gold level requires that the Tier 1 and Tier 2 goals be met plus at least one individual academic and behavioral SMART goal be established and achieved for students not responding to Tier 1 and Tier 2 interventions.

This book focuses on developing a Champion Model PBIS System at the Bronze level; therefore, this chapter focuses on establishing and achieving school-wide academic and behavioral goals and the actions of a school PBIS team in support of this work. We have found that most schools establish Tier 1 academic goals as a part of their regular school business; however, many of these schools have not established a school-wide behavior goal or deployed processes directly aligned to their school-wide goals.

**So what is a Tier 1 academic goal?** A Tier 1 academic goal is a school-wide academic SMART (Strategic and Specific, Measurable, Attainable/Achievable, Results-Oriented and Relevant, and Time-Bound) goal drafted by the PBIS team based on school-wide academic data and finalized with staff input and critical mass support.

**So what is a Tier 1 behavioral goal?** A Tier 1 behavioral goal is a school-wide behavioral SMART goal drafted by the PBIS team based on school-wide behavior data and finalized with staff input and critical mass support.

A PBIS Champion Model System uses multiple data sources to establish at least one school-wide academic goal and one school-wide behavioral goal, develops actions directly aligned toward achieving established goals, executes the actions, and then monitors and communicates progress toward achieving the goals. In this chapter, we have provided you with a series of questions for your system to consider and an action plan template to support future work (see Appendix A-5: School-Wide Academic and Behavioral Goals Questionnaire in Appendix Resources A). The questionnaire should be used to assess the current state of your system relative to academic and behavioral goals, and the sample organizing template can be used to help your system plan, execute, and monitor next-step, high-leverage work. There is nothing magical about this specific template. If you already have an action plan template that works well for your system, then use it. The important aspect of Category C is that the system establishes at least one school-wide academic SMART goal and one school-wide behavioral SMART goal that includes specific indicators of success, develops actions directly aligned to those goals, executes the actions, and then monitors progress toward goal attainment. This should be a focus for the PBIS team—to lead this work.

**Who should complete the questionnaire?** The PBIS team should complete the questionnaire. If you do not have a PBIS team established just yet, the site administrator with his or her leadership/school team should complete the questionnaire.

| School-Wide Academic and Behavioral Goals Questionnaire | | |
| --- | --- | --- |
| Questions to Consider . . . | Academic Yes or No | Behavioral Yes or No |
| 1. Does our school have a PBIS team that reviews school-wide *academic/behavioral* data (e.g., leadership team)? | | |
| 2. Does our PBIS team meet at least monthly to review school-wide *academic/behavioral* data? | | |
| 3. Does our PBIS team have access to school-wide *academic/behavioral* data? | | |
| 4. Has our PBIS team established at least one school-wide *academic/behavioral* SMART goal based on assessed need? | | |
| 5. Can every staff member at our school articulate our school-wide *academic/behavioral* SMART goals? | | |
| 6. Does our school have a process to monitor progress toward meeting our established school-wide *academic/behavioral* SMART goals? | | |
| 7. Does our school have a plan to communicate progress made on school-wide *academic/behavioral* SMART goals to our staff, students, and the community? | | |
| 8. Does our school PBIS team use an agenda that focuses discussion on our school-wide *academic/behavioral* SMART goals? | | |

*Note:* See School-Wide Academic and Behavioral Goals Questionnaire in Appendix A-5, Appendix Resources A.

### SCHOOL-WIDE ACADEMIC AND BEHAVIORAL GOALS ACTIONS TO CONSIDER BASED ON DATA ANALYSIS . . .

- Establish a PBIS team that reviews school-wide academic and behavioral data.
- Calendar the PBIS team to meet at least monthly to review school-wide academic and behavioral data.
- Administration provides the PBIS team access to school-wide academic and behavioral data and prepares and provides reports requested by the PBIS team at every meeting.

*(Continued)*

(Continued)

- PBIS team develops at least one school-wide academic and behavioral SMART goal (including indicators of success) based on school-wide data and with staff input.
- PBIS team regularly (every staff meeting) educates staff about the academic and behavioral SMART goals and communicates progress toward goal attainment.
- PBIS team establishes a process and schedule to help monitor the school-wide academic and behavioral goals (monthly, quarterly, by semester).
- PBIS team selects and uses an agenda (i.e., PBIS Team Meeting Minutes and Problem- Solving Action Plan Form) or some type of formal process to discuss school-wide (academic and behavioral) SMART goals and next steps.
- Gather input and feedback from students, staff, and community regarding the focus of school-wide academic and behavioral goals.
- Build staff knowledge of the *why* and *how* of implementing interventions or initiatives in support of achieving school-wide academic and behavioral SMART goals.
- Keep the school-wide academic and behavioral SMART goals a priority (e.g., write them into your school site plan).

Analyze your School-Wide Academic and Behavioral Goals Questionnaire data. What did the data tell you? Based on the information gained from this analysis and the suggested actions to consider, what next-step or high-leverage actions will your school team take in support of the work—which is to: establish at least one school-wide academic and behavioral SMART goal that includes specific indicators of success, develop directly aligned actions to accomplish those goals, execute actions, and monitor progress toward goal attainment?

Actions

For each action, state when the action will start, person(s) responsible, evidence of the action, and the target completion date. As you monitor these actions, include the date as each is completed.

| Action | Timeline (month/ year to start action) | Person(s) Responsible | Evidence | Target Completion Date (month/ year) | Actual Completion Date (month/ year) |
|---|---|---|---|---|---|
| 1. | | | | | |
| 2. | | | | | |
| 3. | | | | | |
| 4. | | | | | |

If your system has already established a school-wide academic goal and a school-wide behavioral goal, then use the following tools (Comparing Our School-Wide Academic Goal With SMART Goal Characteristics and Comparing Our School-Wide Behavioral Goal With SMART Goal Characteristics**)** to compare your goals with SMART goal criteria. If your system does not have a school-wide goal in one or both of these areas (academic and behavioral), use the SMART criteria to establish your goals.

## COMPARING OUR SCHOOL-WIDE ACADEMIC GOAL WITH SMART GOAL CHARACTERISTICS

Does our academic goal have each of the following characteristics?

- ✓ **S**trategic and **S**pecific
- ✓ **M**easurable
- ✓ **A**ttainable/**A**chievable
- ✓ **R**esults-Oriented and **R**elevant
- ✓ **T**ime-Bound

*(See sample Appendix A-6 in Appendix Resources A)*

❧❧

| SMART Goal Characteristics | Our School-Wide Academic Goal: *Write your school-wide academic goal.* |
|---|---|
| Strategic and Specific | *Write the portion of your school-wide academic goal evidencing that it is strategic and specific.* |
| Measurable | *Write the portion of your school-wide academic goal evidencing that it is measurable.* |
| Attainable/ Achievable | *Explain why you believe your school-wide academic goal is attainable/achievable.* |
| Results-Oriented and Relevant | *Write the portion of your school-wide academic goal evidencing that it is results-oriented and relevant.* |
| Time-Bound | *Write the portion of your school-wide academic goal evidencing that it is time-bound.* |

❧❧

❧❧

The final version of our school-wide academic SMART goal is . . .

_____

_____

_____

❧❧

## COMPARING OUR SCHOOL-WIDE BEHAVIOR GOAL WITH SMART GOAL CHARACTERISTICS

Does our behavior goal have each of the following characteristics?

- ✓ **S**trategic and **S**pecific
- ✓ **M**easurable
- ✓ **A**ttainable/**A**chievable
- ✓ **R**esults-Oriented and **R**elevant
- ✓ **T**ime-Bound

*(See sample Appendix A-7 in Appendix Resources A)*

| SMART Goal Characteristics | Our School-Wide Behavioral Goal: *Write your school-wide behavioral goal.* |
|---|---|
| Strategic and Specific | *Write the portion of your school-wide behavioral goal evidencing that it is strategic and specific.* |
| Measurable | *Write the portion of your school-wide behavioral goal evidencing that it is measurable.* |
| Attainable/ Achievable | *Explain why you believe your school-wide behavioral goal is attainable/achievable.* |
| Results-Oriented and Relevant | *Write the portion of your school-wide behavioral goal evidencing that it is results-oriented and relevant.* |
| Time-Bound | *Write the portion of your school-wide behavioral goal evidencing that it is time-bound.* |

The final version of our school-wide behavioral goal is . . .

_____

_____

_____

# Lessons Learned, Case Studies, and Bringing It All Together

**T**his chapter begins with a few lessons learned by staff who have been trained in the development of our Positive Behavior Interventions and Supports (PBIS) Champion Model System, representing more than 300 schools. Next, four case studies from various education environments (elementary school, middle school, high school, and an alternative education setting) are presented; all four schools have been recognized as Bronze PBIS Champion Model Schools. The case studies focus on some of the challenges the schools faced and the actions they took to move their system to a Tier 1 Bronze PBIS Champion Model System. This chapter concludes with the opportunity for you to bring it all together and make sense of your current context, in light of the PBIS Champion Model System, and decide on your course of action. What do you need to do next?

---

**Lessons Learned**

- Administrator attendance at all PBIS meetings is essential. The PBIS team members feel like their ideas are supported and heard.
- All members of the PBIS team must deliver consistent key messages regarding PBIS—common language must be used,
- When alternative discipline is used appropriately and communication with staff about discipline decisions is timely, staff commitment is strengthened and sustained.
- When the PBIS team holds itself accountable for its action plan steps, students and staff experience consistent implementation and follow-through.
- Feedback must be gathered on an ongoing, regular basis from students and staff to maximize PBIS implementation success and gain commitment from all.
- The allocation of protected time for the PBIS team to meet monthly is essential for consistent implementation and staff messaging about progress.
- Establishing school-wide academic and behavioral SMART goals is essential to the evaluation of a PBIS system and its effectiveness.

---

## CASE STUDIES

As you read these case studies, reflect on the ABCs of developing a Tier 1 Bronze PBIS Champion Model System: Category A—10 PBIS Markers, Category B—School-Wide Characteristics, and Category C—School-Wide Academic and Behavioral Goals and the Work of the PBIS Team. These schools faced various challenges, and the leadership (administrative, teacher, and/or student) took specific actions to move the school from its current state to a more desired future—recognized as a Tier 1 Bronze Champion Model School. Consider the following focus questions as you read and reflect on each case:

- What specific actions were taken that supported the development of a strong Tier 1 PBIS foundation?
- What category did these actions address (A, B, or C)?
- What actions might you consider a *red* flag and indicate that something may need to be addressed?

### ELEMENTARY SCHOOL CASE STUDY: SUNFLOWER ELEMENTARY SCHOOL

*I knew my school was at a Bronze level when I had a parent call me and tell me that as her child was saying her good night prayers, she added her school-wide PBIS expectations to them before saying amen!*

—Sunflower Elementary School principal

Sunflower Elementary is part of a K–12 unified school district. As part of a district-wide improvement strategy, each school was charged with implementing a proactive systems approach to establishing the behavioral supports and social culture needed for all students in the school to achieve social, emotional, and academic success—otherwise known as PBIS. Sunflower Elementary was known for deploying a strong Response to Intervention (RTI) approach for students with learning needs but did not have a proactive systems approach for behavioral support—PBIS.

The school principal at the time of the initial design and implementation of PBIS lacked clarity on what an effective PBIS system looked like and sounded like. The primary action expected at Sunflower Elementary in response to the district's charge of implementing PBIS was to develop a PBIS team made up of diverse members of the school. The principal did not establish a PBIS team; however, he did develop, with no input from others, school-wide behavior expectations that were used only during school rallies. Further development and deployment of PBIS was basically put on hold until a leadership change occurred.

As soon as the new principal arrived, one of his first actions was to establish a PBIS team on campus and schedule time monthly for the team to meet and discuss implementation of Tier 1 PBIS. He gave an overview of PBIS and asked individuals interested in being members of the PBIS team to identify themselves. He told the members that this would count as one of their adjunct duties for the school. Soon the principal had seven members on the PBIS team, and he structured time at every staff meeting for them to share the intended next-step actions regarding PBIS implementation and gather staff input relative to this work. At first, the staff was hesitant and did not really understand PBIS, but the principal assured the staff that everything they would be asked to do would be practical, modeled, and practiced. He provided the PBIS team time to research options of school-wide expectations and structured time at a staff meeting for the team to facilitate a process to establish school-wide behavior expectations. The staff voted on the expectations, Strive for Five: Be Respectful, Be Safe, Work Peacefully, Strive for Excellence, and Follow Directions. A school-wide hand signal was developed as a visual method for teaching students and staff the expectations. Every day for a three-week period in the cafeteria during lunch, administration and cafeteria staff taught and practiced with students the meaning of Strive for Five.

All students and staff were involved in a school-wide passport day event where students walked from setting to setting (cafeteria, office, hallway, bathroom, classroom, library, computer lab, playground, bus) throughout the school to learn what the school-wide behavior expectations looked like in each setting. Students received a stamp in their passport for each location based on their participation and learning. Teachers identified a few students at the end of the PBIS passport teaching whom they perceived as needing additional small group instruction. This perception was based on student behavior and participation at each of the stations. These students were provided reteaching opportunities in small group settings.

Strive for Five tickets were awarded to students caught demonstrating the school-wide behavior expectations. Initially, this recognition system began with administrators weekly placing tickets in staff members' boxes, and staff were asked to give out at least ten tickets a week; however, the system evolved to staff giving out as many as they thought were warranted, and they had access to additional tickets in the office. School-wide announcements were made every morning, and a pledge was developed that the students heard and recited in their classrooms every morning. Every Friday, office staff, custodial staff, administration, and cafeteria staff recognized five students from each classroom for outstanding behavior in various settings. As recognition for this behavior, students selected something from the treasure box in the office.

A school-wide behavior goal was established, which was to decrease suspensions by 50 percent compared to the previous school year (equated to a total of thirty-two suspension incidents). The PBIS team educated the staff regarding this goal and met with the yard duty staff to ensure that active supervision was taking place. During the first year of PBIS implementation, suspensions decreased by more than 75 percent, and to date, the school has maintained similar discipline data. During year three of PBIS implementation, the school was a National Blue Ribbon School nominee. School-wide behavior expectations were part of the foundation at Sunflower Elementary as they were integrated into every aspect of the school. Administration created a culture for positive behaviors and alternative discipline that were effective for students. For example, if students were involved in an altercation, the discipline or consequence was not sending students home for three days. Instead, the consequence/intervention for the behavior was participation in Hands Off Academy: attending four to five sessions where the students worked together on resolving the issues, fulfilling requirements of a behavior contract to earn school privileges back, and passing a required behavior exam. Sunflower Elementary focused on teaching behavior similar to how they teach academics and guaranteeing that every student and staff member on campus clearly understood the meaning of Strive for Five.

## MIDDLE SCHOOL CASE STUDY: TULIP MIDDLE SCHOOL

*I knew my school was at a Bronze level when our school PBIS team stopped letting the few negative staff members interrupt implementation and presentations at staff meetings.*

—Tulip Middle School principal

Tulip Middle School began PBIS implementation with the following principal actions: A PBIS team was established; however, the principal did not attend the PBIS meetings. The principal individually created school-wide behavior expectations, which he then distributed to staff. His key message to staff about PBIS was that suspensions would decrease. However, there was no mention of PBIS as providing proactive behavioral supports to create a climate conducive for social, emotional, and academic success. These actions resulted in staff who could not articulate the school-wide behavior expectations, no positive recognition for students demonstrating behavior in alignment with school-wide expectations, and skeptical staff regarding PBIS implementation. As time went on, the PBIS team became discouraged with trying to deal with negative staff members at every staff meeting without administrative support and, therefore, one day dismantled as a team.

A year later, there was a change in the Tulip Middle School administrative team. This administrative team tried to establish a new PBIS team; however, they encountered difficulty. No staff member wanted to participate. The administrative team talked with staff to gain a better understanding of staff apprehension and negative feelings about committing to the implementation of PBIS. The PBIS team in the school was reestablished and included additional influential staff members. The administrative team created time for the reestablished PBIS team to meet and do the work as well as created PBIS task force teams, which included all other staff members who wanted to provide input and feedback related to the work. These actions supported the beginning work of the PBIS team, which was to assist the system in establishing school-wide behavior expectations, known as ROAR: Respect, On Task, Attitude, and Responsibility. The PBIS team developed a teaching video with the intended purpose of teaching ROAR, the school-wide behavior expectations, in all classrooms. The video included staff explaining the expectations and what they looked like in each setting. In addition, during classroom and school-wide rally settings, staff demonstrated non-examples of the expected behaviors (the wrong way), and students demonstrated examples of the expected behavior (the right way). Friday drawings were established for students who received "caught being good" tickets and for staff who demonstrated the school-wide behavior expectations (nominated by students). The student leadership team announced student and staff names during morning announcements.

The actions that prompted the greatest change in faculty commitment to PBIS were related to the way in which staff understood discipline and the way it was approached. In the initial implementation of PBIS, staff felt as if PBIS meant no discipline because they were not aware of discipline consequences and there was no process to monitor these consequences. For example, staff would give detention to students, but detention consisted of students sitting unsupervised on a bench in the middle of a quad at the school. This discipline consequence was not effective, and teachers felt that students were not provided with reteaching opportunities and resolution. With staff input, the referral process was updated, and teachers were given options for consequences/interventions. The school staff established consequences/interventions both inside and outside of the classroom and for teacher-handled minor behaviors (e.g., disrespect, defiance, tardiness). The administration developed a toolkit of consequences/interventions for major behaviors (e.g., repeated bullying, fighting, gravity of violation). The new leadership also started positive initiatives throughout the school such as beautification projects and team building to reunite the staff focused on always doing what is in the best interest of students.

Changing staff mind-set due to their initial experiences with PBIS implementation has been time-intensive work and continues to be a focus of the PBIS team. The PBIS team and staff have worked hard to decrease the number of office discipline referrals for major incidents, and the number of suspensions decreased 50 percent during their first year of implementation of the PBIS Champion Model System.

## HIGH SCHOOL CASE STUDY: ROSE HIGH SCHOOL

*I knew my school was at a Bronze level when during a football team bus ride, the captain of the team resolved a conflict between a few team members by reminding them to demonstrate the school-wide PBIS expectations and the team listened.*

—Rose High School principal

Rose High School began implementation of PBIS in partnership with another high school in the same district. The administration found it challenging to get a PBIS team established and the message out to such a large staff and student body. However, the principal relentlessly supported the PBIS team and coach and provided them with the opportunity (e.g., substitute coverage) to plan and implement their initiatives. During the initial stages of implementation, the PBIS team spoke about PBIS to the entire staff; however, the staff was hesitant because they did not want to add anything to their already full plate. The administration used school data to demonstrate how business as usual—the current operating system for trying to change student behavior—was not working. The principal highlighted school policies that were not working toward achieving their goals of keeping students in school learning. Specifically, the policy regarding Saturday School was reviewed. Students who ditched class were assigned Saturday School. If a student was assigned Saturday School and did not attend (which most students did not attend), the student was given an automatic three days of suspension, ultimately giving the student permission now to stay home. The consequence did not change student behavior, and the suspension data of the school increased by over 40 percent.

The principal provided time for the PBIS team to speak to the entire staff and each department about the easy-to-implement plans and steps to help alleviate the concern of additional staff work. The key message was that PBIS implementation would be a preventative approach and provide support to create a culture of positive behavior and increase academic achievement in the school. However, the PBIS team quickly learned that they were going to need the help of students to influence staff and students on the campus as to why this was so important. Data was then collected from several classrooms of students about behavior and safety needs of the school, and this information was shared with the staff. In addition, a student team was selected to help teach the established school-wide behavior expectations, otherwise known as CLAWS: Come Prepared, Live Responsibly, Act Safely, Work Together, and Show Respect. The students, in collaboration with the PBIS coach, developed a process for teaching the entire student body about the school-wide behavior expectations, which included learning incentives. They developed a school-wide teaching day with incentives for students who demonstrated learning of the school-wide expectations. All staff were provided a one-page teaching guide, detailing the school-wide behavior expectations—CLAWS—with an explanation of each expectation. Staff members were asked to share this information with each of their classes and to inform their students that there would be a day during the week when incentives would be awarded to students who could articulate the school-wide expectations. The PBIS coach worked with the leadership students to gather input on how to teach the behavior expectations to the student body. The PBIS coach also gave the leadership students the task of watching PBIS videos online prior to providing their feedback. She referenced a few high school PBIS videos on YouTube she liked and allowed the students time during class to watch and reflect on them as a leadership team. On a designated day of the week, leadership students were divided throughout the school campus at lunchtime with boxes of donated incentives. It was a simple task; students would come up and articulate what CLAWS stood for, and if they got it correct, they received a small incentive. If students were incorrect, they received a practice sheet explaining the meaning of CLAWS. After this initial effort to teach the school-wide expectations—CLAWS—to the entire student body, CLAWS was embedded in all morning announcements. Teachers were also provided with a written document, explaining CLAWS, that they were expected to include in their syllabi.

Every teacher was also asked to review the school-wide expectations with the students in their classrooms. In addition, weekly raffle tickets were provided for staff to award to students who demonstrated the highlighted school-wide expectation (or theme) of the week. For example, week one focused on Come Prepared (from CLAWS), so teachers were given raffle tickets to award to students whose behaviors demonstrated this expectation—coming prepared to class. Every Friday during morning announcements, leadership students pulled winners from awarded raffle tickets for the given week.

The PBIS team collected input from department heads regarding how to continue embedding CLAWS in the classroom. The principal asked each department chair to allocate time for the PBIS team members to come and share at a department meeting. Staff was also educated at every staff meeting about alternatives to suspensions being used for students on a case-by-case basis with teacher input. Rose High School decreased suspensions by 63 percent during its first year of PBIS implementation by addressing the ABCs outlined in the Tier 1 Bronze PBIS Champion Model System.

## ALTERNATIVE EDUCATION CASE STUDY: GARDENIA ALTERNATIVE EDUCATION SCHOOL

*I knew my school was at a Bronze level when my staff began to utilize the school-wide incentive system in place of the punitive system we had in place for ten years.*

—Gardenia Alternative Education School principal

Welcome to Gardenia Alternative Education School prior to Tier 1 Bronze PBIS Champion Model System implementation. What would you have seen and heard as you walked onto campus? The school had a negative point system set up for behavior. For example, staff members were constantly on the walkie-talkies subtracting points from students for not doing the right thing (e.g., pull up your pants minus one point from student X). The discipline system was punitive only and not working—not supportive in creating behavioral supports and a social culture needed for all students to achieve social, emotional, and academic success. When the administration announced that the discipline system was not producing the outcomes for students that was needed, the staff was very hesitant about changing anything because they had been used to using a specific method of punitive discipline for such a long time and were not familiar with other approaches. However, when the data was shown to the staff about increases in suspensions, expulsions, and referrals out of the classroom, a few staff members agreed to be part of the PBIS team. Gardenia Alternative Education School had never established a PBIS team that met on a regular basis and had never used behavior data to analyze and discuss what was and was not working. This fact amazed many inside and outside this school environment, as this was a school that dealt with the most severe discipline problems.

The newly established PBIS team constantly educated themselves on effective methods for building positive relationships with their students and gathered input and feedback from their students regarding discipline approaches that work and those that do not. The PBIS team asked a few students to speak during a staff meeting about what they thought would work for them and their peers. The PBIS coach also visited every classroom and collected input from students on what they thought the school-wide behavior expectations should be. This input was used to create school-wide expectations called Gardenia Respect: respect yourself, respect property, and respect others. The PBIS team selected a few influential students to be members of the PBIS team, and this expanded team visited every classroom for five to ten minutes to educate students about the behavior expectations and gather input about incentives. A Gardenia Alternative Education School student expressed, "No one has ever asked us what incentives motivate us or what we are interested in."

Students also introduced the idea of sponsoring a poster contest for the purpose of producing a logo that best illustrated the Gardenia Respect expectations. The contest winner's logo serves as the official school-wide expectations logo and is illustrated on all communications regarding the school-wide expectations.

The PBIS team, in collaboration with the school psychologist, developed a Tier 1 school-wide incentive program—the Principal 200 Club—to recognize students who demonstrate the school-wide expectations. This incentive program is easy to implement and strongly supported by students and staff. The Principal 200 Club consists of a chart (20 rows of 10) numbered from 1 to 200 that is posted in the school office. The PBIS team created incentive tickets that are awarded to students weekly in class who demonstrate Gardenia Respect. Each student who receives a ticket is invited to redeem the ticket in the office during break and after school for a small prize as well as to pull a number (1–200) out of a box. The student writes his/her name on the Principal 200 Club chart that corresponds to the number pulled out of the box. Once a row is completely filled (either horizontally or vertically), the entire row of students decides on a group incentive that they all receive from a list of choices. Student input was used to develop the list of incentives. For example, a group decided between the incentive of extra basketball time or extra lunchtime.

Gardenia Alternative Education School decreased suspensions by 40 percent during their first year of PBIS implementation. Administration and staff focused on building a solid Tier 1 foundation—a proactive, preventative behavior system approach rather than a negative, reactive system. The culture shifted not only from a reactionary discipline system to a proactive system but to a culture focused on building strong relationships between students and staff, gathering student and staff input and feedback to inform next-step decisions—especially in regard to incentives that were of interest to students and emphasizing recognition of desired behaviors over recognition of negative behaviors.

## BRINGING IT ALL TOGETHER

This book focused on the building blocks of a Tier 1 Bronze PBIS Champion Model System, otherwise known as, the ABCs of Tier 1. Designed as an interactive guide to help you assess, learn, process, and action plan your next steps toward Bronze Level implementation, now let's bring it all together.

| Tier 1—Bronze PBIS Champion Model System Progress Summary Sheet | | |
|---|---|---|
| Category A: Tier 1 PBIS Markers | What is our score? | What is one tactic or action we will deploy to make progress in this area? If the highest score was earned, *what will we do to sustain this high level?* |
| Marker 1: Establish and Operate an Effective PBIS Team | | |
| Marker 2: Establish and Maintain Faculty/Staff Commitment | | |
| Marker 3: Establish and Deploy Effective Procedures for Dealing with Discipline | | |
| Marker 4: Establish a Data Entry Procedure and Design an Analysis Plan | | |
| Marker 5: Establish a Set of School-Wide Behavior Expectations and Rules | | |

| Category A: Tier 1 PBIS Markers | What is our score? | What is one tactic or action we will deploy to make progress in this area? If the highest score was earned, *what will we do to sustain this high level?* |
|---|---|---|
| Marker 6: Establish a Behavior Reward/Recognition Program | | |
| Marker 7: Develop and Deliver Lesson Plans for Teaching School-Wide Behavior Expectations and Rules | | |
| Marker 8: Develop and Deploy a School-Wide PBIS Implementation Plan | | |
| Marker 9: Establish Classroom Systems— Routines/ Procedures | | |
| Marker 10: Establish and Execute an Evaluation Plan | | |
| Category B: Tier 1 School-Wide Characteristics | What is our score? | What is one tactic or action we will deploy to make progress in this area? If the highest score was earned, *what will we do to sustain this high level?* |
| School-Wide Characteristic 1: Existence of School-Wide Expectations | | |

*(Continued)*

(Continued)

| Category B: Tier 1 School-Wide Characteristics | What is our score? | What is one tactic or action we will deploy to make progress in this area? If the highest score was earned, *what will we do to sustain this high level?* |
|---|---|---|
| School-wide Characteristic 2: Visibility of School-Wide Behavior Expectations and Rules in Multiple Settings | | |
| School-wide Characteristic 3: Student Knowledge of School-Wide Behavior Expectations | | |
| School-Wide Characteristic 4: Staff Knowledge of School-Wide Behavior Expectations and Other Tier 1 PBIS Markers | | |
| **Category C: Tier 1 School-Wide Academic and Behavioral Goals and the Work of the PBIS Team** | **What is our final version of our school-wide goals?**<br><br>**What is one tactic or action we will deploy to support progress toward achieving the goal?** | |
| School-Wide academic SMART goal. . . | | |
| School-Wide behavioral SMART goal is. . . | | |

# Appendix Resources A

Appendix A-1. Complete Benchmarks of Quality Scoring Rubric (Adapted Version)

Appendix A-2. PBIS Videos and School Visit Contact Information

Appendix A-3. Behavior Grid

Appendix A-4. On-Site PBIS Tier 1 Walkthrough Form (Adapted Version and Scoring Scale)

Appendix A-5. School-Wide Academic and Behavioral Goals Questionnaire

Appendix A-6. Comparing a School-Wide Academic Goal With SMART Goal Characteristics

Appendix A-7. Comparing a School-Wide Behavioral Goal With SMART Goal Characteristics

## Appendix A-1. Complete Benchmarks of Quality (Revised) and Scoring Rubric

| Marker 1: Establish and Operate an Effective PBIS Team | 3 points | 2 points | 1 point | 0 points | Score |
|---|---|---|---|---|---|
| 1. The PBIS team has administrative support. | Administrator(s) attended training, play an active role in the PBIS process, actively communicate their commitment, support the decisions of the PBIS team, and attend **all** team meetings. | Administrator(s) support the process, take as active a role as the rest of the PBIS team, and/or attend **most** meetings. | Administrator(s) support the process but don't take as active a role as the rest of the PBIS team, and/ or attends **only a few** meetings. | Administrator(s) **do not** actively support the PBIS process. | __/3 |
| 2. The PBIS team has regular meetings (at least monthly). | The PBIS team meets monthly (**minimum of nine** one-hour meetings each school year). | | The PBIS team meetings are not consistent (**five to eight** monthly meetings each school year). | The PBIS team seldom meets (**fewer than five** monthly meetings during the school year). | __/2 |
| 3. The PBIS team has established a clear mission/purpose. | | | The PBIS team **has** a written purpose/mission statement for the team (commonly completed on the cover sheet of the action plan). | There is **no** purpose/ mission statement written for the PBIS team. | __/1 |

| Marker 2: Establish and Maintain Faculty/Staff Commitment | 3 points | 2 points | 1 point | 0 points | Score |
|---|---|---|---|---|---|
| 4. The faculty/staff members are aware of behavior problems across campus through regular data sharing. | | Data regarding school-wide behavior **are** shared with faculty/staff members monthly (**minimum of eight times** per year). | Data regarding school-wide behavior **are occasionally** shared with faculty/staff members (**three to seven times** per year). | Data **are not** regularly shared with faculty/staff members. Faculty/staff members may be given an update **zero to two times** per year. | __/2 |
| 5. The faculty/staff members are involved in establishing and reviewing goals. | | **Most** faculty/staff members participate in establishing PBIS goals (i.e., surveys) on at least an annual basis. | **Some** of the faculty/staff members participate in establishing PBIS goals (i.e., surveys) on at least an annual basis. | The faculty/staff members **do not** participate in establishing PBIS goals. | __/2 |
| 6. Faculty/staff feedback is obtained throughout year. | | The faculty/staff **is given** opportunities to provide feedback, to offer suggestions, and to make choices in every step of the PBIS process (via staff surveys, voting process, suggestion box, etc.). Nothing is implemented without the majority of faculty/staff approval. | The faculty/staff **is given some** opportunities to provide feedback, to offer suggestions, and to make some choices during the PBIS process. However, the team also makes decisions without input from faculty/staff members. | The faculty/staff **is rarely given** the opportunity to participate in the PBIS process (**fewer than two times** per school year). | __/2 |

*(Continued)*

(Continued)

| Marker 3: Establish and Deploy Effective Procedures for Dealing With Discipline | 3 points | 2 points | 1 point | 0 points | Score |
|---|---|---|---|---|---|
| 7. **The discipline process is described in narrative format or depicted in graphic format.** | | The PBIS team **has** established clear written procedures that lay out the process for handling both major and minor discipline incidents (**includes** crisis situations). | The PBIS team **has** established clear written procedures that lay out the process for handling both major and minor discipline incidents (**does not include** crisis situations). | The PBIS team **has not** established clear written procedures for discipline incidents and/or there is no differentiation between major and minor incidents. | __/2 |
| 8. **The discipline process includes documentation procedures.** | | | **A procedure exists** to document and track both major and minor behavior incidents (i.e., form, database entry, file in room, etc.). | **No procedure exists** to document and track major and minor behavior incidents (i.e., form, database entry, file in room, etc.). | __/1 |
| 9. **The discipline referral form includes information useful in decision making.** | | Information on the referral form includes **all** of the required fields: Student's name, date, time of incident, grade level, referring faculty/staff member, location of incident, gender, problem behavior, possible motivation, others involved, and administrative decision. | The referral form includes **all** of the required fields, but also includes unnecessary information that is not used to make decisions and may cause confusion. | The referral form **lacks** one or more of the required fields **or does not** exist. | __/2 |

| | | | | | Score |
|---|---|---|---|---|---|
| **10. The problem behaviors are defined.** | Written documentation exists that includes clear definitions of **all** behaviors listed. | **All** of the behaviors are defined, **but some** of the definitions are unclear. | **Not all** behaviors are defined or **some** definitions are unclear. | **No** written documentation of definitions exists. | __/3 |
| **11. The major/minor behaviors are clearly differentiated.** | | **Most** faculty/staff members are clear about which behaviors are staff managed and which are sent to the office (i.e., appropriate use of office referrals). Those behaviors are clearly defined, differentiated, and documented. | **Some** faculty/staff members are unclear about which behaviors are staff managed and which are sent to the office (i.e., appropriate use of office referrals), or no documentation exists. | Specific major/minor behaviors **are not** clearly defined, differentiated, or documented. | __/2 |
| **12. There is a suggested array of appropriate responses to major (office-managed) problem behaviors.** | | | There is evidence that **all** administrative faculty/staff members are aware of and use an array of predetermined appropriate responses to major behavior problems. | There is evidence that **some** administrative faculty/staff members are not aware of, or do not follow, an array of predetermined appropriate responses to major behavior problems. | __/1 |

*(Continued)*

| Marker 4: Establish a Data Entry Procedure and Design an Analysis Plan | 3 points | 2 points | 1 point | 0 points | Score |
|---|---|---|---|---|---|
| 13. **The data system is used to collect and analyze office discipline referral data.** | The database can quickly output data in graph format and allows the team access to **all** of the following information: average referrals per day per month, by location, by problem behavior, by time of day, by student, and compare between years. | **All** of the information can be obtained from the database (average referrals per day per month, by location, by problem behavior, by time of day, by student, and compare between years), **though it may not be** in graph format, may require more faculty/staff time to pull the information, or require faculty/staff time to make sense of the data. | Only **partial** information can be obtained (lacking either the number of average referrals per day per month, location, problem behavior, time of day, student, and compare patterns between years). | The data system is **not able** to provide any of the necessary information the team needs to make school-wide decisions. | ___/3 |
| 14. **Additional data are collected (i.e., attendance, grades, faculty/staff attendance, surveys) and used by the school-wide PBIS team.** | | | The PBIS team collects and considers data other than discipline data to help determine progress and successes (i.e., attendance, grades, faculty/staff attendance, school surveys, etc.). | The PBIS team does **not** collect or consider data other than discipline data to help determine progress and successes (i.e., attendance, grades, faculty/staff attendance, school surveys, etc.). | ___/1 |

| | 3 points | 2 points | 1 point | 0 points | Score |
|---|---|---|---|---|---|
| **15. Data are analyzed by team at least monthly.** | | Data **are** printed, analyzed, and put into graph format or other easy-to-understand format by a member of the PBIS team **monthly (minimum).** | Data **are** printed, analyzed, and put into graph format or other easy-to-understand format by a team member **less than once a month.** | Data are **not** analyzed. | ___/2 |
| **16. Data are shared with team and faculty/staff members monthly (minimum).** | | Data are shared with the PBIS team and faculty/staff members **at least once a month.** | Data are shared with the PBIS team and faculty/staff members **less than once a month.** | Data **are not** reviewed by the PBIS team and shared with faculty/staff members. | ___/2 |
| **Marker 5: Establish a Set of School-Wide Behavior Expectations and Rules** | **3 points** | **2 points** | **1 point** | **0 points** | **Score** |
| **17. Three to five positively stated school-wide behavior expectations are posted around the school.** | **Three to five** positively stated school-wide behavior expectations are visibly posted around the school. Areas posted include the classroom and a minimum of three other school settings (i.e., cafeteria, hallway, front office, etc). | **Three to five** positively stated behavior expectations are visibly posted in **most** important areas (i.e., classroom, cafeteria, hallway), but one area may be missed. | **Three to five** positively stated behavior expectations **are not** clearly visible in common areas. | Behavior expectations **are not** posted or there are too few or too many behavior expectations. | ___/3 |

*(Continued)*

(Continued)

| Marker 5: Establish a Set of School-Wide Behavior Expectations and Rules | 3 points | 2 points | 1 point | 0 points | Score |
|---|---|---|---|---|---|
| 18. **Behavior expectations apply to both students and faculty/staff members.** | PBIS team **has** communicated that behavior expectations apply to **all students and all faculty/staff members.** | The PBIS team **has** behavior expectations that apply to **all students and all faculty/staff members but haven't** specifically communicated that they apply to faculty/staff members as well as students. | Behavior expectations refer **only** to student behavior. | There are **no** behavior expectations. | __/3 |
| 19. **Rules are developed and posted for specific settings (settings where data suggested rules are needed).** | | Rules are posted in **all** of the most problematic areas in the school. | Rules are posted in **some but not all** of the most problematic areas of the school. | Rules **are not** posted in any of the most problematic areas of the school. | __/2 |
| 20. **Rules are linked to behavior expectations.** | | | When taught or enforced, faculty/staff members **consistently** link the rules with the school-wide behavior expectations. | When rules and expectations are taught or enforced, faculty/staff members **do not consistently** link the rules with the school-wide behavior expectations, and/or rules are taught or enforced separately from behavior expectations. | __/1 |

| | 3 points | 2 points | 1 point | 0 points | Score |
|---|---|---|---|---|---|
| **21. Faculty/staff members are involved in development of behavior expectations and rules.** | **Most** faculty/staff members were involved in providing feedback/input into the development of the school-wide behavior expectations and rules (i.e., survey, feedback, initial brainstorming session, election process, etc.). | | **Some** faculty/staff members were involved in providing feedback/input into the development of the school-wide behavior expectations and rules. | Faculty/staff members **were not** involved in providing feedback/input into the development of the school-wide behavior expectations and rules. | __ /2 |
| **Marker 6: Establish a Behavior Reward/Recognition Program** | **3 points** | **2 points** | **1 point** | **0 points** | **Score** |
| **22. A system of rewards has elements that are implemented consistently across campus.** | The reward system guidelines and procedures **are** implemented consistently across campus. Almost all members of the school are participating appropriately (**at least 90 percent** participation). | The reward system guidelines and procedures **are** implemented consistently across campus. However, some faculty/staff members choose not to participate or participation does not follow the established criteria (**at least 75 percent** participation). | The reward system guidelines and procedures **are not** implemented consistently because several faculty/staff members choose not to participate or participation does not follow the established criteria (**at least 50 percent** participation). | There is no identifiable reward system or a large percentage of faculty/staff members are not participating (**less than 50 percent** participation). | __ /3 |
| **23. A variety of methods are used to reward students.** | | The school **uses** a variety of methods to reward students (i.e., cashing in tokens/points). There | The school **uses** a variety of methods to reward students, **but** students do not have access to a | The school **uses only one** set method to reward students (i.e., tangibles only) or there | __ /2 |

*(Continued)*

(Continued)

| Marker 6: Establish a Behavior Reward/ Recognition Program | 3 points | 2 points | 1 point | 0 points | Score |
|---|---|---|---|---|---|
| | | should be opportunities that include tangible items, praise/recognition, and social activities/events. Students with few/many tokens/points have equal opportunities to cash them in for rewards. However, larger rewards are given to those earning more tokens/points. | variety of rewards in a consistent and timely manner. | are no opportunities for children to cash in tokens or select rewards. Only students who meet the quotas actually get rewarded; students with fewer tokens cannot cash in tokens for a smaller reward. | |
| 24. Rewards are linked to behavior expectations and rules. | Rewards are provided for behaviors that **are** linked to the behavior expectations/rules, and faculty/staff members **verbalize** the appropriate behavior when giving rewards. | Rewards are provided for behaviors that **are** linked to the behavior expectations/rules, and faculty/staff members **sometimes verbalize** appropriate behaviors when giving rewards. | Rewards are provided for behaviors that **are** linked to the behavior expectations/rules, but faculty/staff members **rarely** verbalize appropriate behaviors when giving rewards. | Rewards **are** provided for behaviors that **are not** linked to the behavior expectations/rules. | —/3 |
| 25. Rewards are varied to maintain student interest. | | The rewards are varied throughout the year and **reflect** students' interests (i.e., consider the student age, culture, gender, and ability level to maintain student interest). | The rewards are varied throughout the school year but **may not** reflect students' interests. | The rewards **are not** varied throughout the school year and **do not** reflect student's interests. | —/2 |

| | 3 points | 2 points | 1 point | 0 points | Score |
|---|---|---|---|---|---|
| **26. The ratio of acknowledgment to corrections is high.** | The ratio of teacher reinforcement of appropriate behavior to correction of inappropriate behavior is **high** (i.e., 4:1). | The ratio of teacher reinforcement of appropriate behavior to correction of inappropriate behavior is **moderate** (i.e., 2:1). | The ratio of teacher reinforcement of appropriate behavior to correction of inappropriate behavior is **about the same** (i.e., 1:1). | The ratio of teacher reinforcement of appropriate behavior to correction of inappropriate behavior is **low** (i.e., 1:4). | ___/3 |
| **27. The students are involved in identifying/ developing incentives.** | | | The students **are often** involved in identifying/ developing incentives. | The students **are rarely** involved in identifying/ developing incentives. | ___/1 |
| **28. The system includes incentives for faculty/staff members.** | | The system **includes** incentives for faculty/staff members, and they **are** delivered consistently. | The system **includes** incentives for faculty/staff members, but they **are not** delivered consistently. | The system **does not** include incentives for faculty/staff members. | ___/2 |
| **Marker 7: Develop and Deliver Lesson Plans for Teaching School-Wide Behavior Expectations and Rules** | **3 points** | **2 points** | **1 point** | **0 points** | **Score** |
| **29. A behavioral curriculum includes teaching behavior expectations and rules.** | | Lesson plans **were** developed and used to teach behavior expectations and rules. | Lesson plans were developed and used to teach behavior expectations but **were not** developed for rules or vice versa. | Lesson plans **have not** been developed or used to teach behavior expectations or rules. | ___/2 |

*(Continued)*

| Marker 7: Develop and Deliver Lesson Plans for Teaching School-Wide Behavior Expectations and Rules | 3 points | 2 points | 1 point | 0 points | Score |
|---|---|---|---|---|---|
| **30. Lessons include examples and non-examples.** | | | Lesson plans **include** both examples of appropriate behavior and examples of inappropriate behavior. | Lesson plans give **no** specific examples or non-examples of appropriate behavior or there are no lesson plans. | __/1 |
| **31. Lessons use a variety of teaching strategies.** | | Lesson plans **are** taught using at least three different teaching strategies (i.e., modeling, role-playing, videotaping). | Lesson plans have been introduced using **fewer than** three teaching strategies. | Lesson plans **have not** been taught or do not exist. | __/2 |
| **32. Lessons are embedded into subject area curriculum.** | | **Nearly all** teachers embed behavior teaching into subject area curriculum on a daily basis. | **About 50 percent** of teachers embed behavior teaching into subject area curriculum or embed behavior teaching fewer than three times per week. | **Less than 50 percent** of all teachers embed behavior teaching into subject area curriculum or only occasionally remember to include behavior teaching in subject areas. | __/2 |
| **33. Faculty/staff and students are involved in development and delivery of behavioral curriculum.** | | | Faculty/staff and students **are** involved in the development and delivery of lesson plans to teach behavior expectations and rules for specific settings. | Faculty/staff and students **are not** involved in the development and delivery of lesson plans to teach behavior expectations and rules for specific settings. | __/1 |

| | 3 points | 2 points | 1 point | 0 points | Score |
|---|---|---|---|---|---|
| 34. Strategies to share key features of school-wide PBIS plan with families/community are developed and implemented. | | | The PBIS plan **includes** strategies to reinforce lessons with families and the community (i.e., after-school programs teach expectations, newsletters offer tips for meeting expectations at home). | The PBIS plan **does not include** strategies to be used by families and the community. | __/1 |
| **Marker 8: Develop and Deploy a School-Wide PBIS Implementation Plan** | | | | | **Score** |
| 35. A curriculum to teach components of the discipline system to all faculty/staff members is developed and used. | | The PBIS team scheduled time to present and train faculty/staff members on the discipline procedures and data system **including** checks for accuracy of information or comprehension. **Training included all components:** referral process (flowchart), definitions of problem behaviors, explanation of major vs. minor forms, and how the data will be used to guide the PBIS team in decision making. | The PBIS team scheduled time to present and train faculty/staff members on the discipline procedures and data system, **but there were no** checks for accuracy of information or comprehension. **Training did not include all components** (i.e., referral process (flowchart), definitions of problem behaviors, explanation of major vs. minor forms, and how the data will be used to guide the PBIS team in decision making. | Faculty/staff members either were not trained or were given the information **without** formal introduction and explanation. | __/2 |

*(Continued)*

(Continued)

| Marker 8: Develop and Deploy a School-Wide PBIS Implementation Plan | 3 points | 2 points | 1 point | 0 points | Score |
|---|---|---|---|---|---|
| 36. Plans for training faculty/staff members to teach students behavior expectations/rules and rewards are developed, scheduled, and delivered. | | The PBIS team scheduled time to present and train faculty/staff on lesson plans to teach students behavior expectations and rules **including** checks for accuracy of information or comprehension. **Training included all components:** plans to introduce the behavior expectations and rules to all students, explanation of how and when to use formal lesson plans, and how to embed behavior teaching into daily curriculum. | The PBIS team scheduled time to present and train faculty/staff on lesson plans to teach students behavior expectations and rules **but there were no** checks for accuracy of information or comprehension. **Training didn't include all components:** plans to introduce behavior expectations and rules to all students, explanation of how and when to use formal lesson plans, and how to embed behavior teaching into daily curriculum. | Faculty/staff members either were not trained or were not given the information **without** formal introduction and explanation. | ___/2 |
| 37. A plan for teaching students behavior expectations/rules/rewards is developed, scheduled, and delivered. | Students are introduced/taught **all** of the following: school-wide behavior expectations, rules for specific settings, reward system guidelines. | Students are introduced/taught **two** of the following: school-wide behavior expectations, rules for specific settings, reward system guidelines. | Students are introduced/taught only **one** of the following: school-wide behavior expectations, rules for specific settings, reward system guidelines. | Students are not introduced/taught **any** of the following: school-wide behavior expectations, rules for specific settings reward system guidelines. | ___/3 |

| | | | |
|---|---|---|---|
| **38. Booster sessions for students and faculty/staff members are planned, scheduled, and implemented.** | Booster sessions **are** planned and delivered to reteach faculty/staff/students at least once in the year and additionally at times when the data suggest problems by an increase in discipline referrals per day per month or a high number of referrals in a specified area. Behavior expectations and rules are reviewed with students regularly (at least 1 time per week). | Booster sessions **are not** utilized fully. For example: booster sessions are held for students but not staff; booster sessions are held for faculty/staff members but not students; booster sessions are not held but behavior expectations and rules are reviewed at least weekly with students. | Booster sessions for students and faculty/staff members **are not** scheduled/planned. Behavior expectations and rules are reviewed with students once a month or less. | ___/2 |
| **39. The schedule for rewards/incentives for the year is planned.** | | There **is a** clear plan for the type and frequency of rewards/incentives to be delivered throughout the year. | There **is no** plan for the type and frequency of rewards/incentives to be delivered throughout the year. | ___/1 |
| **40. The plans for orienting incoming faculty/staff members and students are developed and implemented.** | The PBIS team **has** planned for and carries out the introduction of school-wide PBIS and training of new staff and students throughout the school year. | The PBIS team **has** planned for the introduction of school-wide PBIS and training of either new students or new faculty/staff members **but does not** include plans for training both, or the team has plans but has not implemented them. | The PBIS team **has not** planned for the introduction of school-wide PBIS and training of new staff or students. | ___/2 |

*(Continued)*

| Marker 8: Develop and Deploy a School-Wide PBIS Implementation Plan | 3 points | 2 points | 1 point | 0 points | Score |
|---|---|---|---|---|---|
| 41. **The plans for involving families/ community are developed and implemented.** | | | The PBIS team **has** planned the introduction to and on-going engagement in school-wide PBIS for families/ community (i.e., newsletter, brochure, PTA, open-house, team membership, etc.). | The PBIS team has **not** introduced school-wide PBIS to families/ community. | ___/1 |

| Marker 9: Establish Classroom Systems— Routines/Procedures | 3 points | 2 points | 1 point | 0 points | Score |
|---|---|---|---|---|---|
| 42. **Classroom rules are defined for each of the school-wide behavior expectations and are posted in classrooms.** | | Evident in most classrooms (**more than 75 percent** of classrooms). | Evident in many classrooms (**at least 50 to 75 percent** of classrooms). | Evident in only a few classrooms (**fewer than 50 percent** of classrooms). | ___/2 |
| 43. **Classroom routines and procedures are explicitly identified for activities where problems often occur (e.g., entering class, asking questions, sharpening pencil, using restroom, dismissal).** | | Evident in most classrooms (**more than 75 percent** of classrooms). | Evident in many classrooms (**at least 50 to 75 percent** of classrooms). | Evident in only a few classrooms (**fewer than 50 percent** of classrooms). | ___/2 |

| | | | |
|---|---|---|---|
| 44. **Expected behavior routines in classrooms are taught.** | Evident in most classrooms (**more than 75 percent** of classrooms). | Evident in many classrooms (**at least 50 to 75 percent** of classrooms). | Evident in only a few classrooms (**fewer than 50 percent** of classrooms). | ___/2 |
| 45. **Classroom teachers use immediate and specific praise.** | Evident in most classrooms (**more than 75 percent** of classrooms). | Evident in many classrooms (**at least 50 to 75 percent** of classrooms). | Evident in only a few classrooms (**fewer than 50 percent** of classrooms). | ___/2 |
| 46. **Acknowledgement of students demonstrating adherence to classroom rules and routines occurs more frequently than acknowledgement of inappropriate behaviors.** | Evident in most classrooms (**more than 75 percent** of classrooms). | Evident in many classrooms (**at least 50 to 75 percent** of classrooms). | Evident in only a few classrooms (**fewer than 50 percent** of classrooms). | ___/2 |
| 47. **Procedures exist for tracking classroom behavior problems.** | Evident in most classrooms **more than 75 percent** of classrooms). | Evident in many classrooms (**at least 50 to 75 percent** of classrooms). | Evident in only a few classrooms (**fewer than 50 percent** of classrooms). | ___/2 |
| 48. **Classrooms have a range of consequences/ interventions for problem behavior that are documented and consistently delivered.** | Evident in most classrooms (**more than 75 percent** of classrooms). | Evident in many classrooms (**at least 50 to 75 percent** of classrooms). | Evident in only a few classrooms (**fewer than 50 percent** of classrooms). | ___/2 |

*(Continued)*

(Continued)

| Marker 10: Establish and Execute an Evaluation Plan | 3 points | 2 points | 1 point | 0 points | Score |
|---|---|---|---|---|---|
| 49. **Students and faculty/staff members are surveyed about PBIS.** | | Students and faculty/staff members **are surveyed** at least annually (i.e. items on climate survey or specially developed PBIS plan survey), and information **is used** to address the PBIS plan. | Students and staff members **are surveyed** at least annually (i.e.. items on climate survey or specially developed PBIS plan survey), but information **is not used** to address the PBIS plan. | Students and staff members **are not** surveyed. | __/2 |
| 50. **Students and faculty/staff members can identify behavior expectations and rules.** | | **Almost all** students and faculty/staff members can identify the school-wide behavior expectations and rules for specific settings (can be identified through surveys, random interviews, etc.), and **at least 90 percent** know/ use. | **Many** students and faculty/staff members can identify the school-wide behavior expectations and rules for specific settings (**at least 50 percent** know/use). | **Few** students and faculty/ staff members can identify the school-wide behavior expectations and rules for specific settings or no evaluation is conducted in this area (**less than 50 percent** know/use). | __/2 |
| 51. **Faculty/staff members use referral process (including which behaviors are office managed vs. which are teacher managed) and forms appropriately.** | **Almost all** faculty/staff members know the procedures for responding to inappropriate behavior, use forms as intended, and fill them out correctly (can be identified by reviewing completed forms, staff surveys, etc.), and **at least 90 percent** know/use. | **Many** of the faculty/staff members know the procedures for responding to inappropriate behavior, use forms as intended, and fill them out correctly (**at least 75 percent** know/use). | **Some** of the faculty/staff members know the procedures for responding to inappropriate behavior, use forms as intended, and fill them out correctly (**at least 50 percent** know/use). | **Few** faculty/staff members know the procedures for responding to inappropriate behavior, use forms as intended, and fill them out correctly, or no evaluation is conducted in this area (**less than 50 percent** know/use). | __/3 |

| | Almost all faculty/staff members understand identified guidelines for the reward system and are using the reward system appropriately (can be identified by reviewing reward token distribution, surveys, etc.), and **at least 90 percent** understand/use. | Many of the faculty/staff understand identified guidelines for the reward system and are using the reward system appropriately (**at least 75 percent** understand/use). | Some of the faculty/staff members understand identified guidelines for the reward system and are using the reward system appropriately (**at least 50 percent** understand/use). | Few faculty/staff members understand and use identified guidelines for the reward system or evaluation is not conducted at least annually in this area or staff knowledge and use of the reward system is not assessed (**less than 50 percent** understand/ use). | |
|---|---|---|---|---|---|
| **52. Faculty/staff members use reward system appropriately.** | | | | | __/3 |
| **53. Outcomes (behavior problems, attendance, and morale) are documented and used to evaluate PBIS plan.** | There is a plan for collecting data to evaluate PBIS outcomes, **most** data are collected as scheduled, and data are used to evaluate PBIS plan. | There is a plan for collecting data to evaluate PBIS outcomes, **some** of the scheduled data have been collected, and data are used to evaluate PBIS plan. | There is a plan for collecting data to evaluate PBIS outcomes; however **nothing** has been collected to date. | There is **no** plan for collecting data to evaluate PBIS outcomes. | __/3 |

**Total Score:**

__/107

*Note: The goal is 80 percent or higher. Divide your total points by the points possible to get the percentage.*

## *Appendix A-2. PBIS Videos and School Visit Contact Information*

| **PBIS Video List** |
| --- |
| What Is PBIS? |
| www.pbis.org/swpbs_videos/school_examples.aspx |
| Active Supervision |
| https://vimeo.com/35272436 |
| Tardy Project |
| www.google.com/search?q=pbis+tardy+project&ie=UTF-8&oe=UTF-8&hl=en&client=safari |
| Show Me My Planner (This one is related to reminding students to use their planners to stay organized.) |
| https://vimeo.com/33794024 |
| Bathroom Expectations (This is the bathroom expectation video, "I Can't Fight This Feeling.") |
| https://vimeo.com/88004531 |
| **School Visit Contact Information** |
| Jessica Hannigan, Ed.D.<br>Website: Pbischampionmodelsystem.com<br>E-mail: Jessica@pbischampionmodelsystem.com |

# Appendix A-3. Behavior Grid

## Red Hawks S.O.A.R.
Reagan's Behavior Matrix

**Voice Levels: 0–3**
0 – Silent
1 – Whisper
2 – Speaking voice
3 – Outdoor voice

| S.O.A.R. in all locations | Classrooms | Hallways | Playground | Cafeteria | Bathroom | Library | Office |
|---|---|---|---|---|---|---|---|
| **S is for Self-Control** | *Keep hands and feet to yourself<br>*Use materials appropriately<br>*Use a quiet voice | *Be aware of others<br>*Face forward in line<br>*Walk at all times | *Keep hands and feet to yourself<br>*Beware of activities around you<br>*Listen for whistle to stop | *Walk at all times<br>*Stay seated with your feet on the floor<br>*Stand in line<br>*Wait patiently | *Walk at all times<br>*Keep hands and feet to yourself<br>*Use a quiet voice | *Use space safely<br>*Keep shelves neat<br>*Use own space<br>*Use quiet voice | *Walk quietly<br>*Sit silently & appropriately on office furniture<br>*Be polite to office staff |
| **O is for on-Task** | *Be on time<br>*Follow directions<br>*Listen attentively<br>*Be willing to participate and answer questions | *Listen to teachers directions<br>*Be in the right place at the right time | *Follow rules<br>*Line up when called<br>*Face forward in line<br>*Stay in line when walking in and out of buildings | *Eat food carefully<br>*Throw away all trash/trays<br>*Clean up eating area | *Use facilities appropriately (water, soap, paper towel)<br>*Return to previous location quickly | *Look at the speaker<br>*Ask questions for clarification<br>*Complete tasks | *Listen to office staff<br>*Complete tasks or errands quickly |

(Continued)

(Continued)

| S.O.A.R. in all locations | Classrooms | Hallways | Playground | Cafeteria | Bathroom | Library | Office |
|---|---|---|---|---|---|---|---|
| **A is for Achievement** | *Give your best effort<br><br>*Be prepared and ready to learn<br><br>*Do your personal best | *Go directly to your destination<br><br>*Walk with a purpose | *Line up quickly to be able to return to class<br><br>*Be alert<br><br>*Strive to make friends with others | *Raise your hands for help<br><br>*Leave your area as clean or cleaner than before | *Use quickly to be able to return to class | *Complete AR goals<br><br>*Know your reading level<br><br>*Leave tables and shelves neat and tidy | *Work quietly on all assignments or tasks |
| **R is for Respect** | *Treat others as you want to be treated<br><br>*Use kind words<br><br>*Help and share with others | *Use a quiet voice<br><br>*Keep hands and feet yourself<br><br>*Respect other students and staff | *Put litter in garbage can<br><br>*Use all equipment properly<br><br>*Invite others to join in<br><br>*Take turns<br><br>*Report problems to an adult | *Use an inside voice<br><br>*Keep hands and feet to yourself<br><br>*Use kind words | *Keep it clean<br><br>*Wait your turn<br><br>*Flush<br><br>*Wash hands | *Turn in all books on time<br><br>*Return computer to "log off"<br><br>*Use a quiet voice | *Enter quietly<br><br>*Wait patiently for an adult<br><br>*Use positive greetings and say "thank you" after being helped |

*Source:* Hannigan, J. (2011). SOAR School-Wide Behavior Matrix. Unpublished.

# Appendix A-4. On-Site PBIS Tier 1 Walkthrough Form (Adapted Version and Scoring Scale)

---

**On-Site PBIS Tier 1 Walkthrough Form**

Purpose: This tool is meant for use as a quick glance when visiting a school to see if School–Wide PBIS is evident. It will allow the observer to provide feedback to the PBIS team and administration.

Observer: _____ School: _____ Date: _____

**School Expectations** _____ _____

_____ _____ _____

**Visibility**

Indicate where School-Wide Behavior **Expectations/Rules Posters** are visible:

Hallways          Main Office          Classrooms          Cafeteria

Gym/Playground          Computer Lab          Other: —————

___/1

___/6

**Classrooms** (Visit 5 classrooms from a variety of classes/grades)
Visit 5 classrooms to determine if **Rules Posters** are visible and
aligned with the School-Wide Behavior Expectations.
*Indicate how many classrooms had visible Rules Posters.*          1   2   3   4   5          ___/5

**Students** (Ask 5 students from a variety of classes\grades)
Ask 5 students if they know the School-Wide Expectations.
*Indicate how many students are able to tell you **all** the expectations.*          1   2   3   4   5          ___/5

**Staff** (Ask 5 staff members the following questions)
Do you have a PBIS team to address behavior/discipline
across campus? *Indicate how many staff know about the team.*          1   2   3   4   5          ___/5

Can you name the School-Wide Behavior Expectations?
*Indicate how many staff are able to tell you **all** the expectations.*          1   2   3   4   5          ___/5

Have you taught the School-Wide Behavior Expectations?
*Indicate how many staff report teaching **all** the behavior expectations.*          1   2   3   4   5          ___/5

Have you seen the school's discipline data this year?
*Indicate how many staff report seeing the data.*          1   2   3   4   5          ___/5

**Additional Comments:**

___/37 TOTAL SCORE

| Total points possible = 37 pts | |
|---|---|
| **On Target** | 30–37 points |
| **Making Progress** | 15–29 points |
| **Need Improvement** | 0–14 points |

---

*Source:* Florida's Positive Behavior Support Project (n.d.).

## *Appendix A-5. School-Wide Academic and Behavioral Goals Questionnaire*

| School-Wide Academic and Behavioral Goals Questionnaire | | |
|---|---|---|
| Questions to Consider . . . | Academic Yes or No | Behavioral Yes or No |
| 1. Does our school have a PBIS team that reviews school-wide *academic/behavioral* data? | | |
| 2. Does our PBIS team meet at least monthly to review school-wide *academic/behavioral* data? | | |
| 3. Does our PBIS team have access to school-wide *academic/behavioral* data? | | |
| 4. Has our PBIS team established at least one school-wide *academic/behavioral* SMART goal based on assessed need? | | |
| 5. Can every staff member at our school articulate our school-wide *academic/behavioral* SMART goals? | | |
| 6. Does our school have a process to monitor progress toward meeting our established school-wide *academic/behavioral* SMART goals? | | |
| 7. Does our school have a plan to communicate progress made on school-wide *academic/behavioral* SMART goals to our staff, students, and the community? | | |
| 8. Does our school PBIS team use an agenda that focuses discussion on our school-wide *academic/behavioral* SMART goals? | | |

# Appendix A-6. Comparing a School-Wide Academic Goal With SMART Goal Characteristics

| SMART Goal Characteristics | **Our School-Wide Academic Goal:** *Write your school-wide academic goal.* |
|---|---|
| | Given informational text reading, at least 80 percent of the students in each grade (K–5) at Champion Elementary School will produce a grade-level or above-level written response for argument/claim/opinion as evidenced by a score of 3 or 4 on all areas of the district rubric (focus/opinion, organization, support/evidence, and language) by the end of the school year. |
| | *Note: Baseline data: K—68 percent; first grade—68 percent; second grade—70 percent; third grade—72 percent; fourth grade—73 percent; fifth grade—74 percent. Rubric scale: 1 = below grade level; 2 = approaching grade level; 3 = at grade level; and 4 = above grade level.* |
| Strategic and Specific | Write the portion of your school-wide academic goal evidencing that it is strategic and specific. |
| | At least 80 percent of the students in each grade (K–5) will produce a grade-level or above-level written response for argument/claim/opinion as evidenced by a score of 3 or 4 on all areas of the district rubric (focus/opinion, organization, support/evidence, and language). |
| | This is a focus of Common Core State Standards (CCSS). |
| Measurable | Write the portion of your school-wide academic goal evidencing that it is measurable. |
| | A score of 3 or 4 is expected on all areas of the district rubric |
| Attainable/ Achievable | Explain why you believe your school-wide academic goal is attainable/achievable. |
| | *Note: Baseline data: K—68 percent; first grade—68 percent; second grade—70 percent; third grade—72 percent; fourth grade—73 percent; fifth grade—74 percent.* |
| | We know what our baseline data is and believe with focused teaching and school-wide use of collective practices learned to address this area of focus, a 10 to 12 percent increase in student learning results is attainable. |
| Results-Oriented and Relevant | Write the portion of your school-wide academic goal evidencing that it is results oriented and relevant. |
| | Results-oriented—A 7 to 12 percent increase in students demonstrating grade-level proficiency compared to the prior year. |
| | Relevant—Focuses on an essential standard and CCSS. |
| Time-Bound | Write the portion of your school-wide academic goal evidencing that it is time-bound |
| | By the end of the school year. |

# Appendix A-7. Comparing a School-Wide Behavioral Goal With SMART Goal Characteristics

| SMART Goal Characteristics | **Our School-Wide Behavioral Goal:** |
|---|---|
| | ***Write your school-wide behavioral goal.*** |
| | By the end of the 2015–2016 school year, the total number of suspensions at Champion Elementary School will decrease at least 40 percent school-wide when compared to 2014–2015 suspension data. |
| | *Note: Baseline data for 2014–2015 is eighty suspensions.* |
| Strategic and Specific | Write the portion of your school-wide behavioral goal evidencing that it is strategic and specific. |
| | By the end of the 2015–2016 school year, the total number of suspensions will decrease at least 40 percent school-wide when compared to 2014–2015 suspension data. |
| | Research has found that students who are suspended or expelled from school tend to do worse academically over time than students who comply with school rules. We believe the more proactive we are in creating positively stated behaviors and implementing a proactive versus a wait-to-misbehave model that leads to a decrease in suspensions, the greater the likelihood that we will increase positive academic outcomes for our students. |
| Measurable | Write the portion of your school-wide behavioral goal evidencing that it is measurable. |
| | The 2015–2016 end-of-year suspension data is compared to 2014–2015 suspension data. We have the baseline data (*eighty suspensions in 2014–2015*) and a data collection system that will give us the end of the year data for 2015–2016. |
| Attainable / Achievable | Explain why you believe your school-wide behavioral goal is attainable/achievable. |
| | *Note: Baseline data: Eighty suspensions.* |
| | We know what our baseline data is and believe with the implementation of a proactive versus a wait-to-misbehave model, a 40 percent decrease in school-wide suspensions in one year is attainable. |
| Results-Oriented and Relevant | Write the portion of your school-wide behavioral goal evidencing that it is results-oriented and relevant. |
| | Results-oriented—40 percent decrease in school-wide suspensions compared to the prior year |

| | |
|---|---|
| | Relevant:<br><br>Research has found that students who were suspended and/or expelled—particularly those who were repeatedly disciplined—were more likely to be held back a grade or to drop out of school than were students not involved in the disciplinary system. When a student was suspended or expelled, his or her likelihood of being involved in the juvenile justice system the subsequent year increased significantly.<br><br>Federal guidelines for schools to improve school climate and discipline include the following: creating positive climates and focus on prevention; developing clear, appropriate, and consistent expectations and consequences to address disruptive student behaviors (improve behavior, increase engagement, boost achievement); and ensuring fairness, equity, and continuous improvement.<br><br>The Local Control Accountability Plan (LCAP) highlights school climate and connectedness through a variety of factors, such as suspension and expulsion rates and other locally identified means. |
| Time-Bound | Write the portion of your school-wide behavioral goal evidencing that it is time-bound.<br><br>By the end of the 2015–2016 school year. |

# Appendix Resources B

These resources are referenced in Chapters 3 and 4 (From the Field—Challenges and Practical Solutions).

Appendix B-1. PBIS Team Meeting Minutes and Problem-Solving Action Plan Form

Appendix B-2. Teacher Behavior Day Script and Passport

Appendix B-3. Minor and Major Behavior Data Tracking Flowcharts

Appendix B-4. Behavior Snapshot E-Mail Example

Appendix B-5. Student Input Form—Establishing Rules for Each Setting

Appendix B-6. Behavior Reward/Recognition Program Insert for Student/Parent Handbook and Faculty Handbook

Appendix B-7. Announcement Template for Teaching School-Wide Behavior Expectations and Rules

Appendix B-8. Year at a Glance—Monthly Action Plan Template

Appendix B-9. Classroom Rules Grid and Affinity Process

Appendix B-10. Positive Behavior Interventions and Supports (PBIS) Data Collection Schedule

Appendix B-11. List of Sample School-Wide Behavior Expectations

Appendix B-12. Pictures/Visuals Posted at Champion Model Schools

Appendix B-13. Positive Behavior Interventions and Supports (PBIS) Teaching Day Memo—Guide for School-Wide Teaching Days

Appendix B-14. Staff Positive Behavior Interventions and Supports (PBIS) Communication Wall—Sample Picture

## *Appendix B-1. PBIS Team Meeting Minutes and Problem-Solving Action Plan Form*

_____ **PBIS Team Meeting Minutes and Problem-Solving Action Plan Form**

**Today's Meeting:** Date: Time: Location: Facilitator: Minute Taker: Data Analyst:
**Next Meeting:** Date: Time: Location: Facilitator: Minute Taker: Data Analyst:

**Team Members (bold are present today)**

| Today's Agenda Items | | Next Meeting Agenda Items | Potential Problems Raised |
|---|---|---|---|
| 01. | 04. | 01. | 01. |
| 02. | 05. | 02. | 02. |
| 03. | 06. | 03. | 03. |

**Administrative/General Information and Issues (Agenda Items)**

| Information for Team, or Issue for Team to Address | Discussion/Decision/Task (if applicable) | Who? | By When? |
|---|---|---|---|
| 01. | | | |
| 02. | | | |
| 03. | | | |
| 04. | | | |
| 05. | | | |
| 06. | | | |

**Problem-Solving Action Plan**

| Precise Problem Statement, based on review of data (What, When, Where, Who, Why) | Solution Actions (e.g., Prevent, Teach, Prompt, Reward, Correction, Extinction, Safety) | Implementation and Evaluation | | |
|---|---|---|---|---|
| | | Who? | By When? | Goal, Timeline, Decision Rule, & Updates |
| | | | | |
| | | | | |
| | | | | |

**Evaluation of Team Meeting (Mark your ratings with an "X")**

| | Our Rating | | |
|---|---|---|---|
| | Yes | So-So | No |
| 1. Was today's meeting a good use of our time? | | | |
| 2. In general, did we do a good job of **_tracking_** whether we're completing the tasks we agreed on at previous meetings? | | | |
| 3. In general, have we done a good job of actually **_completing_** the tasks we agreed on at previous meetings? | | | |
| 4. In general, are the completed tasks having the **_desired effects_** on student behavior? | | | |

## Appendix B-2. Teacher Behavior Day Script and Passport

| Bathroom Passport Day Script | |
|---|---|
| **Teacher or person running the behavior station says the following:** | **Students say the following:** |
| • What are our school-wide behavior expectations? | • Strive for Five: Be Respectful, Be Safe, Work Peacefully, Strive for Excellence, and Follow Directions |
| • When you see this hand, what does it mean?<br><br><br><br>• Show the Strive for Five hand signal to students.<br>• Say it with me: "When you see this hand signal, it means the Strive for Five way." | • It means the Strive for Five way. |
| • When you see this sad face, what does it mean?<br><br><br><br>• Say it with me: "It means this is not the Strive for Five way." | • It means this is not the Strive for Five way. |
| • Now let's practice how we do it the Strive for Five way in the bathroom.<br>    First, let's look at some non-examples in the bathroom:<br>  o Leaving toilet unflushed<br>  o Throwing paper towels on the ground<br>  o Screaming<br>  o Play fighting<br>  o Playing around<br>  o Tagging<br>  o Forgetting to wash your hands | • Have students give a thumbs-up or a thumbs-down after an older student or another teacher demonstrate the wrong-way examples.<br>• Have students talk to an elbow partner about the non-examples in the bathroom. Call on a few students to share. |
| • Now let's look at the Strive for Five examples in the bathroom:<br>  o Keep it clean.<br>  o Wait your turn.<br>  o Flush the toilet.<br>  o Wash hands.<br>  o Use facilities appropriately (water, soap, paper towel).<br>  o Use a quiet voice.<br>*You can call these out one by one, and the students can show you the five signal if they are doing it the Strive for Five way.* | • Have students give a thumbs-up or a thumbs-down after an older student or another teacher demonstrate the right-way examples.<br>• Have students talk to an elbow partner about the Strive for Five way to behave in the bathroom. Call on a few students to share. |

## POSITIVE BEHAVIOR INTERVENTIONS AND SUPPORTS (PBIS) PASSPORT DAY LOCATIONS

| | | |
|---|---|---|
| ☐ Library | ☐ Computer | |
| ☐ Hallway | ☐ Lab | |
| ☐ Playground | ☐ Bathroom | |
| ☐ Cafeteria | ☐ Bus | |
| ☐ Classroom | ☐ PE | |

Grade: _____     Name: _____

Date of Issue: _____

Copyright © 2015 by Corwin. All rights reserved. Reprinted from *The PBIS Tier One Handbook: A Practical Approach to Implementing the Champion Model* by Jessica Djabrayan Hannigan and Linda Hauser. Thousand Oaks, CA: Corwin, www.corwin.com

# Appendix B-3. Minor and Major
# Behavior Data Tracking Flowcharts

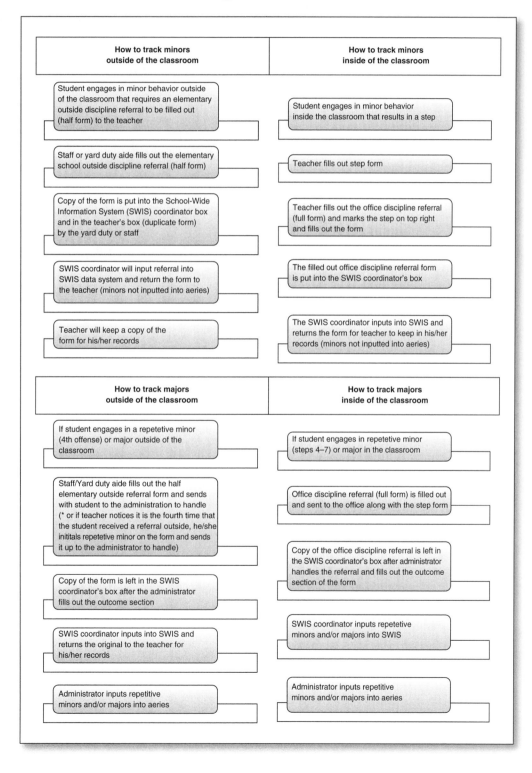

| How to track minors outside of the classroom | How to track minors inside of the classroom |
|---|---|
| Student engages in minor behavior outside of the classroom that requires an elementary outside discipline referral to be filled out (half form) to the teacher | Student engages in minor behavior inside the classroom that results in a step |
| Staff or yard duty aide fills out the elementary school outside discipline referral (half form) | Teacher fills out step form |
| Copy of the form is put into the School-Wide Information System (SWIS) coordinator box and in the teacher's box (duplicate form) by the yard duty or staff | Teacher fills out the office discipline referral (full form) and marks the step on top right and fills out the form |
| SWIS coordinator will input referral into SWIS data system and return the form to the teacher (minors not inputted into aeries) | The filled out office discipline referral form is put into the SWIS coordinator's box |
| Teacher will keep a copy of the form for his/her records | The SWIS coordinator inputs into SWIS and returns the form for teacher to keep in his/her records (minors not inputted into aeries) |

| How to track majors outside of the classroom | How to track majors inside of the classroom |
|---|---|
| If student engages in a repetetive minor (4th offense) or major outside of the classroom | If student engages in repetetive minor (steps 4–7) or major in the classroom |
| Staff/Yard duty aide fills out the half elementary outside referral form and sends with student to the administration to handle (* or if teacher notices it is the fourth time that the student received a referral outside, he/she inititals repetetive minor on the form and sends it up to the administrator to handle) | Office discipline referral (full form) is filled out and sent to the office along with the step form |
| Copy of the form is left in the SWIS coordinator's box after the administrator fills out the outcome section | Copy of the office discipline referral is left in the SWIS coordinator's box after administrator handles the referral and fills out the outcome section of the form |
| SWIS coordinator inputs into SWIS and returns the original to the teacher for his/her records | SWIS coordinator inputs repetetive minors and/or majors into SWIS |
| Administrator inputs repetitive minors and/or majors into aeries | Administrator inputs repetitive minors and/or majors into aeries |

## *Appendix B-4. Behavior Snapshot E-Mail Example*

Dear Staff,

We have noticed a high number of referrals on the playground and in the classroom. Please continue to review the Positive Behavior Interventions and Supports (PBIS) classroom and recess rules daily with your students prior to releasing them. Please let the PBIS team know if you have any suggestions to improve teaching and monitoring behaviors in these areas. We will be recognizing classrooms or periods that have demonstrated an improvement in decreasing the number of referrals this month.

PBIS Team

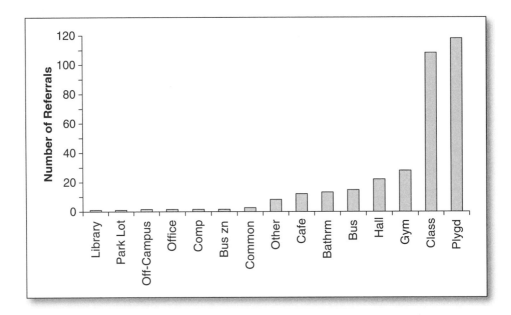

Copyright © 2015 by Corwin. All rights reserved. Reprinted from *The PBIS Tier One Handbook: A Practical Approach to Implementing the Champion Model* by Jessica Djabrayan Hannigan and Linda Hauser. Thousand Oaks, CA: Corwin, www.corwin.com

# Appendix B-5. Student Input Form— Establishing Rules for Each Setting

| Bathroom Behavior | |
|---|---|
| • Provide input on THE WRONG WAY to behave in the bathroom based on what you have seen at your school. | • Provide input on THE RIGHT WAY to behave in the bathroom based on what you have seen at your school. |
| | |

| Classroom Behavior | |
|---|---|
| • Provide input on THE WRONG WAY to behave in the classroom based on what you have seen at your school. | • Provide input on THE RIGHT WAY to behave in the classroom based on what you have seen at your school |
| | |

Copyright © 2015 by Corwin. All rights reserved. Reprinted from *The PBIS Tier One Handbook: A Practical Approach to Implementing the Champion Model* by Jessica Djabrayan Hannigan and Linda Hauser. Thousand Oaks, CA: Corwin, www.corwin.com

## Appendix B-6. Behavior Reward/Recognition Program Insert for Student/Parent Handbook and Faculty Handbook

---

**Strive for Five Recognition System**

- To effectively change student behavior and improve the school climate, the school has developed a reinforcement plan to strengthen and support the Positive Behavior Interventions and Supports (PBIS) model.

**Strive For Five**

- Be Respectful
- Be Safe
- Work Peacefully
- Strive for Excellence
- Follow Directions

**Recognition**

- Students have the opportunity to be recognized for consistently demonstrating positive behavior in all areas of the school.
- Students are recognized with Strive for Five Caught Being Good tickets.
- All staff, including teachers, substitute teachers, main office staff, cafeteria staff, custodians, and bus drivers, award Strive for Five tickets.
- One side of the Strive for Five tickets can be used during Friday snack shack to purchase school incentives or snacks approved by administration. The other half of the ticket is entered in a Strive for Five weekly school-wide drawing. Five winners are selected weekly and recognized over the announcements and are given the opportunity to select a Strive for Five prize from the office treasure box.
- Classrooms are recognized weekly as Strive for Five line winners, Strive for Five Cafeteria winners, Strive for Five Custodian winners, and more: good grades, attendance, Fun Friday elective classes, Positive Behavior Referral home, Positive phone calls home, Teacher choice awards, and Other classroom reward activities.

# Appendix B-7. Announcement Template for Teaching School-Wide Behavior Expectations and Rules

## CLAWS Announcement Schedule

Please start off your announcement every day with the following Grizzly CLAWS pledge:

In order to make _____ High a great place to be, ALL students are expected to come prepared, live responsibly, act safely, work together, and show respect.

**Please announce:** Teachers will be handing out caught showing CLAWS tickets to students demonstrating the CLAWS expectations. Tickets will be collected for a drawing at the end of each week.

|  | Monday | Tuesday | Wednesday | Thursday | Friday |
|---|---|---|---|---|---|
| **Come Prepared Week: March 4–March 8** | • **Wrong Way:** Coming to class without a pencil | • **Wrong Way:** Not completing homework | • **Wrong Way:** Coming late to class | • **Wrong Way:** Leaving backpack at home | • **Wrong Way:** Staying up all night |
|  | • **Right Way:** Having a pencil | • **Right Way:** Turning in homework on time | • **Right Way:** Getting to class on time | • **Right Way:** Bringing what you need to class | • **Right Way:** Being ready to learn |
| **Live Responsibly Week: March 11–March 15** | • **Wrong Way:** Using inappropriate language | • **Wrong Way:** Using drugs | • **Wrong Way:** Walking toward fights and not getting help | • **Wrong Way:** Throwing trash on ground | • **Wrong Way:** Falling behind on assignments in class |
|  | • **Right Way:** Using appropriate language | • **Right Way:** Staying away from drugs; staying focused on goals | • **Right Way:** Walking away and getting help | • **Right Way:** Throwing trash in the garbage can | • **Right Way:** Staying caught up and asking for help when needed |

*(Continued)*

(Continued)

|  | Monday | Tuesday | Wednesday | Thursday | Friday |
|---|---|---|---|---|---|
| **Act Safely Week: March 18–March 22** | • **Wrong Way:** Playing around with hands on | • **Wrong Way:** Seeing someone hurt and not helping | • **Wrong Way:** Hearing about an upcoming fight and not reporting it | • **Wrong Way:** Ignoring students smoking in the bathroom | • **Wrong Way:** Knowing about a group meeting off campus to fight |
|  | • **Right Way:** Keeping hands, feet, and objects to yourself | • **Right Way:** Helping others when they need it | • **Right Way:** Reporting anonymously so that the fight can be prevented | • **Right Way:** Informing an adult about the situation | • **Right Way:** Notifying an adult of the situation so that it can be prevented and no one gets hurt |
| **Work Together Week: April 8–April 12** | • **Wrong Way:** Not collaborating in class with other students | • **Wrong Way:** Not speaking up when someone needs help | • **Wrong Way:** Not completing your part of the group assignment or project | • **Wrong Way:** Refusing teacher help | • **Wrong Way:** Walking by trash on the ground and not helping pick up and throw away |
|  | • **Right Way:** Collaborating and brainstorming with other students | • **Right Way:** Helping others in and out of class setting | • **Right Way:** Being an active member of the group and completing your assigned task on time | • **Right Way:** Taking advantage of the opportunity to get help from the teacher | • **Right Way:** Helping keep the campus clean by picking up trash on the ground |
| **Show Respect Week: April 15–April 19** | • **Wrong Way:** Not responding when greeted | • **Wrong Way:** Giving the teacher attitude | • **Wrong Way:** Talking when the teacher is talking | • **Wrong Way:** Texting and using cell phone during class | • **Wrong Way:** Passing notes in class |
|  | • **Right Way:** Saying hi and smiling when acknowledged by others | • **Right Way:** Letting the teacher know privately that you are having a bad day | • **Right Way:** Listening to the teacher when he/she is speaking to the class | • **Right Way:** Putting the phone away and being engaged in class | • **Right Way:** Taking class notes and participating in class |

Copyright © 2015 by Corwin. All rights reserved. Reprinted from *The PBIS Tier One Handbook: A Practical Approach to Implementing the Champion Model* by Jessica Djabrayan Hannigan and John E. Hannigan. Thousand Oaks, CA: Corwin, www.corwin.com.

## Appendix B-8. Year at a Glance—Monthly Action Plan Template

| Positive Behavior Interventions and Supports (PBIS) Champion Model System Action Plan: Year at a Glance | | |
|---|---|---|
| **What We Need to Do?** | **By What Date?** | **Check Off When Completed** |
| • Baseline PBIS assessments completed<br>• PBIS team meeting<br>•<br>•<br>• | August | |
| • PBIS team meeting<br>•<br>•<br>• | September | |
| • Baseline On-Site PBIS Tier 1 Walkthrough completed<br>•<br>•<br>• | October | |
| • PBIS team meeting<br>•<br>•<br>• | November | |
| • PBIS team meeting<br>•<br>•<br>• | December | |
| • PBIS team meeting<br>•<br>•<br>• | January | |
| • PBIS team meeting<br>•<br>•<br>• | February | |

*(Continued)*

(Continued)

| What We Need to Do? | By What Date? | Check Off When Completed |
|---|---|---|
| • Final On-Site PBIS Tier 1 Walkthrough and assessments completed<br>• PBIS team meeting<br>•<br>•<br>• | March | |
| • PBIS team meeting<br>•<br>•<br>• | April | |
| • PBIS team meeting<br>•<br>•<br>• | May | |
| • PBIS team meeting<br>•<br>•<br>• | June | |

Copyright © 2015 by Corwin. All rights reserved. Reprinted from *The PBIS Tier One Handbook: A Practical Approach to Implementing the Champion Model* by Jessica Djabrayan Hannigan and Linda Hauser. Thousand Oaks, CA: Corwin, www.corwin.com

# Appendix B-9. Classroom Rules Grid and Affinity Process

| Classroom Expectations/Rules<br>*Strive for Five: Be Respectful, Be Safe, Work Peacefully,<br>Strive for Excellence, Follow Directions* | | | |
|---|---|---|---|
| **Routines/<br>Procedures** | **What It Looks Like** | **Right Way Example** | **Wrong Way Example** |
| Transition | • Put/get materials first.<br>• Keep hands to yourself.<br>• Have a plan.<br>• Go directly.<br>• Use your inside voice. | For example, the student quickly gets prepared for the next directed task. | For example, the student starts talking to neighbors and playing inside his/her desk. The student does not have materials ready. |
| Pair share | • Know your assigned partner.<br>• Turn to your assigned partner promptly.<br>• Be able to share what was discussed with your partner. | For example, the student knows who his/her partner is and turns promptly to face partner as directed. | For example, the student does not know who his/her partner is. The student is off topic. |
| Independent practice | • Work quietly and independently on the assigned task.<br>• Use time as planned as directed by the teacher. | For example, the student uses time appropriately and completes tasks independently. The student has a plan after completion of task. | For example, the student talks to partners, does not work on assignment, and is not prepared. |
| Bathroom break | • Arrive promptly to class after Music/Choir. | For example, the student follows bathroom procedures and returns promptly to class. | For example, the student returns after several minutes. The student wanders around campus. |
| Small group pull-back instruction | • Be prepared.<br>• Bring the appropriate materials.<br>• Walk over quietly, and find your seat promptly. | For example, the student gathers needed materials and walks promptly to small group setting. The student is on task. | For example, the student needs to be called to come back to the small group repeatedly. The student comes without materials. |

*(Continued)*

(Continued)

| Routines/Procedures | What It Looks Like | Right Way Example | Wrong Way Example |
|---|---|---|---|
| Whole group instruction | • Keep your eyes on the speaker.<br>• Use materials properly.<br>• Be prepared. | For example, the student has eyes on the speaker, has appropriate materials, and is on task. | For example, the student is playing in his/her desk, has the wrong book out, is distracting neighbors, and is not prepared. |
| Choir/music time | • Return to class promptly after Music/Choir practice. | For example, the student promptly returns to class. | For example, the student takes the long route back to class, talks to friends in the bathroom, and wanders around the school. |
| "I need assistance" | • Raise your hand.<br>• Ask questions if anything is unclear. | For example, the student raises his/her hand to ask for assistance or clarify a task. | For example, the student blurts out comments, does not wait for his/her turn, and repeatedly interrupts the teacher. |
| Homework | • Do your own work.<br>• Turn in homework neatly and on time. | For example, the student is prepared to turn in their homework. | For example, the student copies another student's homework and turns it in. |

## *Appendix B-10. Positive Behavior Interventions and Supports (PBIS) Data Collection Schedule*

**PBIS Data Collection Schedule: What assessments need to be collected throughout the school year to evaluate implementation and effectiveness of PBIS?**

The purpose of collecting PBIS data is to (a) monitor implementation at model PBIS levels and (b) provide data that can demonstrate the effectiveness of PBIS implementation. This chart shows what data are collected throughout the school year.

| Description and Schedule of Collected PBIS Data | First Benchmark (Beginning of the School Year or Beginning of Implementation) | Second Benchmark (End of the School Year or Four Months After Initial Implementation) |
|---|:---:|:---:|
| • **Benchmarks of Quality (BoQ)** completed by PBIS team and coach | X | X |
| • **On-Site PBIS Tier 1 Walkthrough Form** completed by administrator assigned to monitor implementation | X | X |
| • **Progress on School-Wide Behavior SMART Goal:** Data collected based on your school goal (e.g., number of minor/major referrals and number of suspensions/expulsions) | X | X |
| • **Progress on School-Wide Academic SMART Goal:** Data collected based on your school goal (e.g., rubric scores, performance assessment scores, work completion, graduation rates) | X | X |

## *Appendix B-11. List of Sample School-Wide Behavior Expectations*

Positive Behavior Interventions and Supports (PBIS) School Behavior Expectation Samples

- **School expectations:** Strive for Five: Be Respectful, Be Safe, Work Peacefully, Strive for Excellence, Follow Directions

- **School expectations:** 3 Bs: Be Safe, Be Respectful, Be Responsible

- **School expectations:** PRIDE: Prepared, Respectful, Integrity, Demonstrates Self-Discipline, Empathy

- **School expectations:** PRIDE: Positivity, Responsibility, Integrity, Discipline, Excellence

- **School expectations:** The Roadrunner Way: Be Responsible, Be Respectful, Be Safe

- **School expectations:** Lion Laws: Respectful, Responsible, Ready to Learn

- **School expectations:** SOAR: Self-Control, On Task, Achievement, Respect

- **School expectations:** Grizzly CLAWS: Come Prepared, Live Responsibly, Act Safely, Work Together, Show Respect

- **School expectations:** Hornet Respect: Respect Others, Respect Ourselves, Respect Property

## Appendix B-12. Pictures/Visuals Posted at Champion Model Schools

## Appendix B-13. Positive Behavior Interventions and Supports (PBIS) Teaching Day Memo— Guide for School-Wide Teaching Days

### High School PBIS Teaching Expectations Activity

- We are running the activity through our PE classes beginning Monday. Each focus area on the behavior matrix will be a station. It will take three days to get all 1,500 students through the stations. Behavior expectations will be reviewed and modeled by the PBIS team at each station. Once all of the students who are registered have visited each station, first period teachers will pass the behavior matrix out during their first period and do a close activity with them. Once the behavior matrix has been completely filled out, the teachers will put a sticker next to each focus area to show that that student understands the expectation. Completed/stickered matrixes will be stapled into the students' agendas and will be referred to when dealing with disciplinary issues. Students receive a red raffle ticket for participating, and their names will be entered into a raffle for some fabulous school attire store. All new students who register after the walkthrough has been completed will get their very own tour with a member of the PBIS team!

## HIGH SCHOOL

| School-Wide Expectations | | | | |
|---|---|---|---|---|
| **Setting** | **Be Responsible** | **Be Respectful** | **Be Ready** | **Follow Directions** |
| **Classroom** | • Complete classwork. <br> • Bring agenda daily. <br> • Ask questions about the lesson. <br> • Follow the homework policy. | • Respect others' space and belongings. <br> • Use appropriate language and tone of voice (0–2). <br> • Follow the classroom guidelines. | • Be in class and in your seat before the bell rings. <br> • Bring the required materials every day. | • Listen and respond politely to adult directions. <br> • Ask when in doubt. |
| **Quad Area** | • Pick up after yourself, and throw all trash away. <br> • Eat and drink only in designated areas. | • Respect others' space. <br> • Use appropriate language and tone of voice (0–2). | • Upon hearing the dismissal bell, move toward the next destination. | • Listen and respond politely to adult directions. |
| **Bathroom** | • Clean up after yourself. <br> • Report any concerns to the office or an adult. | • Respect others' privacy. <br> • Maintain a clean and graffiti free environment. | • Wait patiently if there is a line. | • Wash your hands. <br> • Throw away paper towels/ trash. |
| **Before/ After School** | • Be in class by 7:45 a.m. <br> • Leave the campus clean. | • Be polite to everyone. <br> • Be conscious of other activities in session. | • Be prepared for before school/ after school activities. | • Walk to your destinations. |
| **Office** | • Be prepared to state your purpose for visiting the office. | • Only the person with a purpose needs to come into the office. | • Form a line and wait quietly for assistance. | • Listen and respond politely to adult directions. |
| **Cafeteria** | • Throw away all trash. <br> • Stack trays. <br> • Vacate the cafeteria when finished eating. | • Say please and thank you. <br> • Use appropriate language toward peers. <br> • Do not throw food. | • Remain in line, and wait patiently. <br> • Have your ID number ready to type in. | • Listen and respond politely to adult directions. <br> • Make lunch account payments before school or during break. |

| School-Wide Expectations | | | | |
|---|---|---|---|---|
| Setting | Be Responsible | Be Respectful | Be Ready | Follow Directions |
| **Gym** | • Be dressed and ready for activity. | • Keep hands and feet to oneself at all times. | • Be in "roll call" before the bell rings. | • Listen and respond politely to adult directions. |
| **Library** | • Arrive with a task in mind.<br>• Report any problems to the librarian. | • Leave food or drink out of the library.<br>• Use appropriate language and tone of voice (0–1). | • Bring your ID card for checking out books. | • Upon entering, "sign-in" the library binder at the desk. |
| **Bus** | • Enter the bus, and find a seat.<br>• Use appropriate language and voice level (0–2). | • Respect others' space and belongings.<br>• Respect the driver's responsibilities. | • Report to your appropriate loading line.<br>• Know your correct route number. | • Listen and respond politely to the bus driver's directions.<br>• Remain fifteen feet away from the road while waiting for the bus. |

Voice Level Key: 0— silent; 1—whisper; 2—normal speaking; 3—slightly raised; 4—outside; 5—emergency.

## Appendix B-14. Staff Positive Behavior Interventions and Supports (PBIS) Communication Wall—Sample Picture

# Appendix Resources C

*Additional Resources*

## EXAMPLE E-MAIL TO STAFF ABOUT HIGH SCHOOL TEACHING DAY

Dear Staff,

We will be having our first Positive Behavior Interventions and Supports (PBIS) teaching day of CLAWS this Wednesday. As you all know, CLAWS stands for Come Prepared, Live Responsibly, Act Safely, Work Together, and Show Respect. During lunchtime on Wednesday, the selected student and teacher helpers will be spread out throughout campus asking students what CLAWS stands for. If the student they ask recites all the expectations correctly, the student will be able to pick out a prize from our collected PBIS donations. If the student cannot recite all school-wide expectations correctly, he/she will be given a practice sheet with the expectations listed to practice for the next school-wide CLAWS teaching day. Please review CLAWS with your classrooms, and let us know if you need any more information ☺.

Thank you,

PBIS Team

Copyright © 2015 by Corwin. All rights reserved. Reprinted from *The PBIS Tier One Handbook: A Practical Approach to Implementing the Champion Model* by Jessica Djabrayan Hannigan and Linda Hauser. Thousand Oaks, CA: Corwin, www.corwin.com

## EXAMPLE BEHAVIOR PLEDGE

School Behavior Pledge

As part of our school family, I pledge to Strive for

Five by being respectful, being safe, working peacefully,

striving for excellence, and following directions.

I will be respectful by using words that are kind and

positive.

I will be safe by keeping my hands, feet, and objects to

myself.

I will work peacefully by solving problems peacefully.

I will strive for excellence by accepting the challenge to

become the best that I can be.

I will follow directions by being responsible and staying on

task.

I will Strive for Five.

Copyright © 2015 by Corwin. All rights reserved. Reprinted from *The PBIS Tier One Handbook: A Practical Approach to Implementing the Champion Model* by Jessica Djabrayan Hannigan and Linda Hauser. Thousand Oaks, CA: Corwin, www.corwin.com

# EXAMPLE OFFICE DISCIPLINE REFERRAL THAT ALIGNS WITH POSITIVE BEHAVIOR INTERVENTIONS AND SUPPORTS (PBIS) IMPLEMENTATION

## Discipline Referral

Student: _____ Date: _____ Time: _____ Grade: _____

Staff Reporting: _____ Teacher: _____

### Location

Playground    Cafeteria    Hallway    Restroom    Other _____

**Minor**                                              **Major**

Defiance/Non-compliance/Disrespect                     Harassment/Bullying                Lying/Cheating

Disruption                                             Property Damage/Vandalism          Abusive Language/Profanity

Inappropriate Language                                 Inappropriate Location/Out of Bounds   Major Disruption

Physical Contact/Physical Aggression                   Fighting/Physical Aggression

Property Misuse                                        Major Defiance; disrespect; insubordination

Minor Other                                            Repetitive Minor _____        Other _____

Briefly Describe the incident: _____

**Others Involved** Peers    Staff/Noon Aide    None    Other _____

**Cause of Behavior** Get peer attention    Avoid peers    Get staff attention    Avoid staff    Get item/activity    Avoid item/activity

**Actions Taken** Warned student    Loss of Recess    Informed Teacher    Referred to Office    Other: _____

Copyright © 2015 by Corwin. All rights reserved. Reprinted from *The PBIS Tier One Handbook: A Practical Approach to Implementing the Champion Model* by Jessica Djabrayan Hannigan and Linda Hauser. Thousand Oaks, CA: Corwin, www.corwin.com

## EXAMPLE YARD DUTY EXPECTATIONS

---

### YARD DUTY EXPECTATIONS

**Positive attitude**

**On time**

**Cell phones put away (unless emergency)**

**Active supervision (scanning, movement, positive interactions)**

**Promptly report to locations (zones) as assigned**

**Separated during yard duty**

**Understand outside referral form process (minor and major)**

**Give out positive "caught being good" tickets during yard duty**

**Know all the school-wide behavior expectations in all assigned yard duty settings**

**Provide corrective feedback to students**

**Monthly yard duty meetings with administration**

**Have fun**

---

Copyright © 2015 by Corwin. All rights reserved. Reprinted from *The PBIS Tier One Handbook: A Practical Approach to Implementing the Champion Model* by Jessica Djabrayan Hannigan and Linda Hauser. Thousand Oaks, CA: Corwin, www.corwin.com

# EXAMPLE RECESS BEHAVIOR ASSIGNMENT

---

**Recess Behavior Assignment**

**Why is it inappropriate to play a game like that during recess?**




**What can we do instead next time?**




**How are we going to make sure this does not happen again?**




**Sign off by Administration and Teacher:**




**Signature:** _____

**Signature:** _____

---

Copyright © 2015 by Corwin. All rights reserved. Reprinted from *The PBIS Tier One Handbook: A Practical Approach to Implementing the Champion Model* by Jessica Djabrayan Hannigan and Linda Hauser. Thousand Oaks, CA: Corwin, www.corwin.com

## EXAMPLE POSITIVE REFERRAL

**Elementary School**

**Strive for Five Positive Referral**

| Dear _____ , | Date: |
|---|---|

Today, _____ was an awesome example for others at Elementary. He/she has displayed the following school-wide Strive for Five expectations and has earned this positive referral.

| Being Respectful | Being Safe | Working Peacefully |
|---|---|---|
| Striving for Excellence | Following Directions | |

Teacher Comments:

Administration Comments:

Teacher Signature: _____ Administrator Signature: _____

White: Teacher     Yellow: Student

Copyright © 2015 by Corwin. All rights reserved. Reprinted from *The PBIS Tier One Handbook: A Practical Approach to Implementing the Champion Model* by Jessica Djabrayan Hannigan and Linda Hauser. Thousand Oaks, CA: Corwin, www.corwin.com

## EXAMPLE BEHAVIOR WORKSHEET

### Being Respectful Worksheet

Name: _____

Write a plan on how you can be more respectful.

_____

_____

_____

_____

_____

What happens when you are not respectful?

_____

_____

_____

_____

_____

What makes you a respectful person?

_____

_____

_____

_____

_____

Write three school rules that help everyone to be respectful.

_____

_____

_____

_____

_____

What consequences should be in place for students who are not respectful?

_____

_____

_____

_____

_____

Give me some examples of things that **are** and **are not** respectful.

_____

_____

_____

_____

_____

On the back of this page, make a poster about being respectful.

Copyright © 2015 by Corwin. All rights reserved. Reprinted from *The PBIS Tier One Handbook: A Practical Approach to Implementing the Champion Model* by Jessica Djabrayan Hannigan and Linda Hauser. Thousand Oaks, CA: Corwin, www.corwin.com

# EXAMPLE CONFLICT RESOLUTION AGREEMENT FORM

Date of Meeting: _____

## Disputants

_____          _____

_____          _____

## Referral Source

Administrator/Teacher/Student/Self/Other: _____

## Conflict Information

What is the conflict about?

_____

_____

_____

1. Did we recognize an injustice/violation?   Yes   No  Other _____

2. Did we restore equity? Apology for injustices/violations

Nothing beyond this meeting necessary          Other: _____

3. Future Intentions (Agreement/Contract)

We agreed to prevent the problem from happening again by doing the following:

_____

_____

_____

Student Signatures: _____

Student Signatures: _____

4. Follow-Up Meeting

We agreed to meet again for a follow-up meeting. Follow-up meeting date:

_____

Student Signatures: _____

Student Signatures: _____

Follow-up Results:

_____

_____

_____

## EXAMPLE BEHAVIOR EXAM

Student: _____

Behavior Exam Questions:

1. What happened that put you in this position?

2. What would you do differently if you can go back and change what happened?

3. What did you learn from this experience?

4. How can you assure the administration that you will not be a part of an incident such as this one ever again?

5. How will you assure the student who was a victim of your behavior that he/she does not have to worry about you bothering him or her anymore?

6. How has your behavior impacted others at the school (e.g., teachers, administration, parents, other students)?

Copyright © 2015 by Corwin. All rights reserved. Reprinted from *The PBIS Tier One Handbook: A Practical Approach to Implementing the Champion Model* by Jessica Djabrayan Hannigan and Linda Hauser. Thousand Oaks, CA: Corwin, www.corwin.com

# EXAMPLE OF CONNECTING POSITIVE BEHAVIOR INTERVENTIONS AND SUPPORTS (PBIS) WITH CHARACTER EDUCATION

## Strive for Five With Character

(See the listed monthly character traits to discuss, and have the students write about them for your classroom character wall and library character wall)

*Note: Student of the Month selection is given to the student exhibiting Strive for Five with the character attribute selected for each month.*

August—Caring: Be helpful and kind to others.

September—Responsibility: Be able to be trusted or relied upon or dependable.

October—Respect: Use words that are kind and positive.

November—Citizenship: Help others in the community, school, and home.

December—Trustworthiness: Tell the truth and do what is right.

January—Fairness: Be able to share and take turns and treat all people equally.

February—Kindness: Be caring; you should want to help others.

March—Honesty: Be truthful; do not lie, cheat, or steal.

April—Tolerance: Be willing to accept people and opinions that are different.

May—Courage: Stand up for what is right.

June—Perseverance: Stick to a purpose or aim and do not give up.

## EXAMPLE HIGH SCHOOL CHALLENGES

### Positive Behavior Interventions and Supports (PBIS) High School Challenges

PBIS challenges can be set up for two-month periods or as long as needed. Each challenge needs a goal at the beginning that is messaged out and taught to the student body (needs to be measurable). Updates on progress of goals need to be reported to staff and student body. Rewards for meeting the challenges should be set up accordingly.

| Type of Challenge | Goal of Challenge | Reward for Meeting the Challenge | Messaging Out and Teaching Challenge | Dates of Challenge (You Can Break up in Months or All Year) |
|---|---|---|---|---|
| Nonviolent Days Challenge | Decrease in number of violent days by 50 percent compared to previous school year | Free dress days | Announcements, classroom instruction | August–September |
| Bully-Free Challenge | Decrease student report of bullies in school by 50 percent compared to baseline survey | School dance | Announcements, classroom instruction | October–November |
| Keep the Campus Clean Challenge | Campus rating from custodian is 50 percent better than beginning of the challenge | Rally | Announcements, classroom instruction | January–February |
| Attendance Challenge | Improve attendance by 50 percent | Lunchtime privileges/activities | Announcements, classroom instruction | March–April |

Copyright © 2015 by Corwin. All rights reserved. Reprinted from *The PBIS Tier One Handbook: A Practical Approach to Implementing the Champion Model* by Jessica Djabrayan Hannigan and Linda Hauser. Thousand Oaks, CA: Corwin, www.corwin.com

# EXAMPLE HANDS OFF ACADEMY COVER SHEET AND PROGRESS MONITORING CHART

**Hands Off Academy Date of Attendance:** _____

**Student:** _____

**Grade:** _____ **Teacher:** _____

**Reason for Being Invited:**

_____

_____

**Goal:**

I, _____, will always Strive for Five by _____.

_____

_____

_____

I, _____, have successfully completed Hands Off Academy on _____.

**Administrator Signature:** _____

### Hands-Off Academy—Weekly Self-Monitoring Form

| *Behaviors: How well did I...* | *Previous Week:* |
|---|---|
| **Show respect to adults and students** | **Circle one:** Good Fair Poor |
| **Keep my hands to myself** | **Circle one:** Good Fair Poor |

What worked for you? _____

_____

What didn't work for you? _____

_____

**Contract for this week:**

I, _____, will work on _____

_____ this week in order to meet my behavior goal.

_____

Copyright © 2015 by Corwin. All rights reserved. Reprinted from *The PBIS Tier One Handbook: A Practical Approach to Implementing the Champion Model* by Jessica Djabrayan Hannigan and Linda Hauser. Thousand Oaks, CA: Corwin, www.corwin.com

## EXAMPLE "I NEED BEHAVIOR SUPPORT" FORM

### I Need BEHAVIOR Support

Student: _____ Date: _____

Teacher: _____ Grade: _____

Student strengths/preferences: _____

_____

_____

Area(s) of concern: _____

_____

_____

Strategies I've used to manage behavior: _____

_____

_____

Effectiveness of strategies: _____

_____

_____

Other essential information: _____

_____

_____

| For Office Use Only: |
| :--- |
| Response Date: _____ By Whom? _____ Actions: _____ |
| Revisit By: _____ |

Copyright © 2015 by Corwin. All rights reserved. Reprinted from *The PBIS Tier One Handbook: A Practical Approach to Implementing the Champion Model* by Jessica Djabrayan Hannigan and Linda Hauser. Thousand Oaks, CA: Corwin, www.corwin.com

# EXAMPLE SOCIAL MEDIA EXERCISE AND PLEDGE

## Social Media Exercise and Pledge

What is the purpose of social media (Facebook, Twitter, Instagram, etc.)?

_____

What is cyberbullying?

_____

Are bullying and making inappropriate comments on social media against the law?

_____

Do your messages or pictures disappear when you delete them?

_____

What are five things you are committing to doing to make sure no cyberbullying is happening online?

1. _____
2. _____
3. _____
4. _____
5. _____

I pledge to do my part to stop cyberbullying. I pledge to always think before I post a message or picture that can hurt myself or others. I also pledge to help a friend by notifying an adult or the school if someone is being cyberbullied.

Rewrite the pledge:

_____

Signature: _____ Date: _____

Copyright © 2015 by Corwin. All rights reserved. Reprinted from *The PBIS Tier One Handbook: A Practical Approach to Implementing the Champion Model* by Jessica Djabrayan Hannigan and Linda Hauser. Thousand Oaks, CA: Corwin, www.corwin.com

## EXAMPLE COMMUNITY SERVICE FORM

### Community Service Form

Student: _____ Grade: _____

Date Service Begins: _____

Hours or Days Assigned: _____

_____ Total hours of service assigned

_____ Total days of service assigned

| Date | Location of Service | Time or Days (e.g., 15 minutes or full day) | Staff Initials | Additional Comments |
|------|--------------------|--------------------------------------------|----------------|---------------------|
|  |  |  |  |  |
|  |  |  |  |  |
|  |  |  |  |  |
|  |  |  |  |  |
|  |  |  |  |  |
|  |  |  |  |  |
|  |  |  |  |  |
|  |  |  |  |  |

At the completion of service, an administrator, parent, and the student needs to sign this document.

Administrator Signature: _____

Parent Signature: _____

Student Signature: _____

Copyright © 2015 by Corwin. All rights reserved. Reprinted from *The PBIS Tier One Handbook: A Practical Approach to Implementing the Champion Model* by Jessica Djabrayan Hannigan and Linda Hauser. Thousand Oaks, CA: Corwin, www.corwin.com

# EXAMPLE BEHAVIORAL AND ACADEMIC CENTER LOG

| Morning/Lunch Responsibility<br>Behavioral and Academic Center Log | | | | | | | |
|---|---|---|---|---|---|---|---|
| **Teacher:** | | | | **Grade:** | | | |
| **Student** | **Date** | **Morning (M)<br>Lunch (L)<br>Both (ML)** | **Homework<br>(HW)** | **Classwork<br>(CW)** | **Behavior<br>(B)** | **Present<br>Morning** | **Present<br>Lunch** |
| | | | | | | | |
| | | | | | | | |
| | | | | | | | |
| | | | | | | | |
| | | | | | | | |
| | | | | | | | |
| | | | | | | | |
| | | | | | | | |
| | | | | | | | |
| | | | | | | | |

Copyright © 2015 by Corwin. All rights reserved. Reprinted from *The PBIS Tier One Handbook: A Practical Approach to Implementing the Champion Model* by Jessica Djabrayan Hannigan and Linda Hauser. Thousand Oaks, CA: Corwin, www.corwin.com

## EXAMPLE YOUNGER STUDENT BEHAVIOR FORM

### Thinking About how to "Strive for Five" Behavior Sheets

| Check the expectation that student needs to work on: | Non-Example "WRONG WAY" | Example "RIGHT WAY" |
|---|---|---|
| ☐ Be Respectful | | |
| ☐ Be safe | | |

Copyright © 2015 by Corwin. All rights reserved. Reprinted from *The PBIS Tier One Handbook: A Practical Approach to Implementing the Champion Model* by Jessica Djabrayan Hannigan and Linda Hauser. Thousand Oaks, CA: Corwin, www.corwin.com

# EXAMPLE PE EXPECTATIONS AND RULES

| PE | PE Expectations/Rules<br>Strive for Five: Be Respectful, Be Safe, Work Peacefully, Strive for Excellence, Follow Directions | | |
|---|---|---|---|
| **Procedures / Routines** | **Rules** | **Example** | **Non-Example** |
| Transition | • Put classroom materials away.<br>• Keep your hands to yourself.<br>• Go directly to/from the PE location.<br>• Use your inside voice. | For example, the student quickly gets prepared to go and return from PE. | For example, the student starts talking to neighbors, plays with peers, and gets off task. |
| Line Up Outside Class (*before and after PE*) | • Line up in the designated spot.<br>• Walk quickly and quietly to the PE location. | For example, the student quickly gets into a straight line in the designated spot ready for PE. | For example, the student talks, plays around, gets a drink of water, and gets out of line. |
| Proceed in Line Out to Yard (*before and after PE*) | • Stay in the designated spot.<br>• Remain in line.<br>• Keep your hands to yourself.<br>• Keep your voices quiet. | For example, the student remains in line all the way to the PE location. | For example, the student walks in groups, talks loudly, does not follow directions, and gets out of line. |
| Bathroom Break | • Ask for permission.<br>• Arrive promptly to PE class. | For example, the student follows bathroom procedures and returns promptly to PE class. | For example, the student returns after several minutes. The student wanders around campus. |
| Whole Group PE Instruction | • Keep your eyes on the speaker.<br>• Remain in designated spots.<br>• Use PE equipment properly.<br>• Keep your hands to yourself.<br>• Be prepared. | For example, the student has his/her eyes on the speaker, has appropriate equipment, and is on task. | For example, the student is playing inappropriately, playing with equipment, distracting neighbors, and not following directions. |
| "I Need Assistance" | • Raise your hand.<br>• Ask if something is unclear. | For example, the student raises his/her hand to ask for assistance or clarify a task. | For example, the student blurts out comments, does not wait for his/her turn, and repeatedly interrupts the teacher. |

Copyright © 2015 by Corwin. All rights reserved. Reprinted from *The PBIS Tier One Handbook: A Practical Approach to Implementing the Champion Model* by Jessica Djabrayan Hannigan and Linda Hauser. Thousand Oaks, CA: Corwin, www.corwin.com

## EXAMPLE CAUGHT BEING GOOD TICKET

# Red Hawk Caught Being

# Good Ticket

**S** = Self-Control

**O** = On Task

**A** = Achievement

**R** = Respect

## EXAMPLE POSITIVE BEHAVIOR INTERVENTIONS AND SUPPORTS (PBIS) FACULTY/STAFF SURVEY

Please circle your answer from the following choices:  strongly agree, agree, no opinion, disagree, strongly disagree.

1. The PBIS team has represented the desires of the faculty as a whole.

   Strongly agree    agree    no opinion    disagree    strongly disagree

2. The PBIS team has established a clear mission/purpose.

   Strongly agree    agree    no opinion    disagree    strongly disagree

3. As a faculty/staff member, you are aware of behavior problems across campus.

   Strongly agree    agree    no opinion    disagree    strongly disagree

4. As a faculty/staff member, you are involved in establishing and reviewing goals.

   Strongly agree    agree    no opinion    disagree    strongly disagree

5. Feedback from faculty/staff was obtained throughout the year.

   Strongly agree    agree    no opinion    disagree    strongly disagree

6. Discipline procedures have been adequately described.

   Strongly agree   agree   no opinion   disagree   strongly disagree

7. Discipline referral forms include useful information.

   Strongly agree   agree   no opinion   disagree   strongly disagree

8. Major and minor behaviors are clearly identified/understood.

   Strongly agree   agree   no opinion   disagree   strongly disagree

9. Suggested appropriate responses to major problem behaviors have been made.

   Strongly agree   agree   no opinion   disagree   strongly disagree

10. Student discipline data is adequately reported to faculty/staff.

    Strongly agree   agree   no opinion   disagree   strongly disagree

11. School-wide expectations are adequately posted around school.

    Strongly agree   agree   no opinion   disagree   strongly disagree

12. Rules are developed and posted for specific settings where problems are prevalent.

    Strongly agree   agree   no opinion   disagree   strongly disagree

13. Staff feedback/involvement in expectations/rules is solicited.

    Strongly agree   agree   no opinion   disagree   strongly disagree

14. A system of rewards has elements that are implemented consistently across campus.

    Strongly agree   agree   no opinion   disagree   strongly disagree

15. Rewards are varied to maintain interest.

    Strongly agree   agree   no opinion   disagree   strongly disagree

16. The reward system includes incentives for staff/faculty.

    Strongly agree   agree   no opinion   disagree   strongly disagree

17. Booster sessions for staff are planned, scheduled, and delivered.

    Strongly agree   agree   no opinion   disagree   strongly disagree

18. Faculty/staff are taught how to respond to a crisis situation.

    Strongly agree   agree   no opinion   disagree   strongly disagree

19. Plans for orienting incoming students are implemented.

    Strongly agree    agree    no opinion    disagree    strongly disagree

20. More training is needed to expand on PBIS interventions for the next school year.

    Strongly agree    agree    no opinion    disagree    strongly disagree

What topics would you like to review, revise, or expand on in a PBIS booster session?

Comments/Feedback:

# References

Childs, K. E., Kincaid, D., & George, H. P. (2011). *The revised school-wide PBS Benchmarks of Quality (BoQ).* Evaluation Brief. OSEP Technical Assistance Center on Positive Behavioral Interventions and Supports. Retrieved from http://www. pbis. org/evaluation/evaluation_briefs/mar_11_ (1). aspx

Cohen, R., Kincaid, D., & Childs, E. K. (2007). Measuring school-wide positive behavior support implementation development and validation of the benchmarks of quality. *Journal of Positive Behavior Interventions, 9,* 203–213.

Fabelo, T., Thompson, M. D., Plotkin, M., Carmichael, D., Marchbanks III, M. P., & Booth, E. A. (2011). *Breaking schools' rules: A statewide study of how school discipline relates to students' success and juvenile justice involvement.* Retrieved from Council of State Governments Justice Center website: csgjusticecenter.org/wp-content/uploads/2012/08/Breaking_Schools_Rules_Report_Final.pdf

Fenning, P. A., & Bohanon, H. (2006). School-wide discipline policies: An analysis of discipline codes of conduct. In C. Evertson & C. S. Weinstein (Eds.), *Handbook of behavior management: Research, practice, and contemporary issues* (pp. 1021–1039). Mahwah, NJ: Erlbaum.

Florida's Positive Behavior Support Project. (n.d.). *Description of model schools.* Retrieved from http://flpbs.fmhi.usf.edu/modelschools.asp

George, P. H. (2008, March). *Establishing a system to appropriately identify, assess, and evaluate PBS model/exemplar schools.* Paper presented at the Fifth International Conference on Positive Behavior Support, Chicago, IL. Retrieved from http://www.cde.ca.gov/sp/se/sr/documents/sldeligibltyrti2.doc

Horner, R. H., Sugai, G., & Anderson, C. M. (2010). Examining the evidence base for school-wide positive behavior support. *Focus on Exceptional Children, 42*(8), 1–14.

Kincaid, D., Childs, K., & George, H. (2010, March). *School-wide benchmarks of quality* (Revised). Unpublished manuscript, Tampa, FL.

Lezotte, L. W. (2010). *What effective schools do: Re-envisioning the correlates.* Indianapolis, IN: Solution Tree.

Newton, J. S., Todd, A. W., Algozzine, K. M., Horner, R. H., & Algozzine, B. (2010). *Team-initiated problem solving training manual.* Unpublished training manual. Educational and Community Supports, University of Oregon, Eugene. Retrieved from http://www.papbs.org/filestorage/moduleupload/7_Team%20Initiated%20Problem%20Solving%20Handbook.pdf

Noonan, B., Tunney, K., Fogal, B., & Sarich, C. (1999). Developing student codes of conduct: A case for parent-principal partnership. *School Psychology International, 20,* 289–299.

Skiba, R. J., & Rausch, M. K. (2005). Zero tolerance, suspension, and expulsion: Questions of equity and effectiveness. In C. Evertson & C. S. Weinstein (Eds.), *Handbook of behavior management: Research, practice, and contemporary issues* (pp. 1063–1089). Mahwah, NJ: Erlbaum.

Sugai, G., & Horner, R. H. (2002). The evolution of discipline practices: School-wide positive behavior supports. *Child and Family Behavior Therapy, 24,* 23–50.

# Index

CORWIN
A SAGE Company

**Helping educators make the greatest impact**

**CORWIN HAS ONE MISSION:** to enhance education through intentional professional learning.

We build long-term relationships with our authors, educators, clients, and associations who partner with us to develop and continuously improve the best evidence-based practices that establish and support lifelong learning.